"I THOUGHT PEOPLE LIKE THAT
KILLED THEMSELVES"

"I Thought People Like That Killed Themselves"

LESBIANS, GAY MEN AND SUICIDE

by
Eric E. Rofes

GREY FOX PRESS
San Francisco

Manufactured in the United States of America.

Copyright acknowledgments will be found on page x.

Book design and typography by Turner & Brown, Inc., Santa Rosa, California

Library of Congress Cataloging in Publication Data

Rofes, Eric E., 1954–
   "I thought people like that killed themselves."

   1. Homosexuals, Male—United States—Suicidal behavior—History—20th century.   2. Lesbians—United States—Suicidal behavior—History—20th century. 3. Homosexuality—United States—Public opinion—History—20th century.   I. Title.
HV6546.R63   1983   362.2   82-9301
ISBN 0-912516-70-4   AACR2
ISBN 0-912516-69-0 (pbk.)

To my uncle Allen
who has inspired me with
his integrity and his courage

CONTENTS

ACKNOWLEDGMENTS

This book developed out of an article written for *The Advocate* in 1979 which explored the subject of lesbians, gay men and suicide. Robert McQueen provided guidance and editing for the piece and I thank him for encouraging me to research this topic and for publishing the article. Donald Allen, my editor at Grey Fox Press who has shown great concern for suicide in the gay community as well as tremendous patience and kindly-worded editorial supervision, is credited and thanked for this book's conception and development.

The title paraphrases a remark made by King George V of England, when told that someone he knew quite well was homosexual. He said, "I thought fellows like that shot themselves." (H. Montgomery Hyde : *The Love That Dared Not Speak Its Name* [Boston: Little Brown, 1970], p. 197.)

Research help, suggestions, information and random tips have come to me from many people during the three years I spent researching this book and I want to thank, in particular, Allen Young, Eva Deykin, Jearld Moldenhauer, Dee Michel, Mitzel, Terry Gock, Denise Sudell, John Kyper, Sandy Steingard, Michael Rumaker, Andy Lynn, Hugh Crell, David Hubert, and Corinne Klafter. I wish to also thank the many lesbians, gay men and their friends and families who shared with me their personal experiences with suicide attempts, feelings or ideation, as well as the friends, lovers and families of lesbians and gay men who have committed suicide. Discussing this topic is neither easy nor pleasant and I have been impressed by the ways in which many people have been willing to help my study by sharing their experiences with me.

I wish to thank the staffs of the Boston Public Library and Harvard Medical School Library and Jim Kepner, curator of the National Gay Archives in Los Angeles, for the great assistance they have given me in my researches. Maida Tilchen pursued extensive research work for this book at the Institute for Sex Research in Bloomington, Indiana, and provided constant support and interest in this project. Her insights have been invaluable to my thinking on this subject.

Sally Casper, Bill Fessenden, Annie Fisher, Paula Rofes, Jim Ryan, Cheryl Schwartz, Marge Sherwin, Nancy Walker, and Rose Walton have read the first draft of this book and offered very helpful suggestions concerning its content and perspective. I am particularly thankful for Joe Interrante's suggestions on the first chapter and Jonathan Ehrenworth's guidance on the book's conclusion.

The staff of the Massachusetts Committee for Children and Youth and members of Project Aware and Project Assist were helpful to my understanding the connection between suicidal teenagers and sexuality issues. My friends at *Gay Community News* have nurtured my work and challenged my thinking on many of the issues involved in this book. The children, parents and staff of the Fayerweather Street School where I have taught throughout the time I've researched this book have kept my spirits happy and optimistic. I also thank my friends at Herbie's, Chaps, the Paradise, the One Way, the Brig, the Spike, the D. C. Eagle, the Atlantic House and the Boatslip who are an important network of friendship in my life.

The work of both Sarah Benet and Sally Casper has provided me with special inspiration for working both with suicidal people and with the lesbian and gay male population. Their tremendous energy and dedication to helping depressed and suicidal people have influenced my work and thinking considerably.

The deaths of several colleagues and friends, including David Brill, Ben Campbell, Mel Horne and Jason Klein, occurred during my work on this book and made me particularly aware of the difficult lives and difficult deaths experienced by gay people in our society.

My agent, Helen Rees, has offered me her guidance and professional expertise for which I will be eternally grateful. My friends David Klafter, Emily Friedan, Paul Stein, Linda Brown, Jonathan Silin, Bob Schram, Richard Burns, Dennis Perry, Wendy Gold, Fran Reich, Cheryl Schwartz, Kathryn Stearns, Wayne Weiner, Michael Friedman and Jimmy Cote have supported my work through kind encouragement, helpful suggestions and generally great cooking and conversation.

David Hocker, who has endured the ups and downs inherent in living with someone who is researching the topic of suicide among lesbians and gay men, as well as the joys of life together in a Victorian brownstone, richly deserves medals, trophies and bouquets of beautiful flowers.

—Eric E. Rofes
Boston, Massachusetts
August, 1982

COPYRIGHT ACKNOWLEDGMENTS

Grateful acknowlegment is given for permission to quote from:

"Concerning the Death of Dr. Michael Silverstein, Gay Activist and Friend" by Larry Tate in *The Body Politic* (June, 1977).

Surviving and Other Essays by Bruno Bettelheim, © 1979, Alfred A. Knopf, Inc.

Man's Search for Meaning by Viktor Frankl, © 1962, Beacon Press.

Night Blooming: About Allyn Amundson, edited by Sal Farinella, © 1976, Good Gay Poets.

Ann Landers Talks to Teenagers About Sex by Ann Landers, © 1963, Prentice-Hall, Inc.

The Myth of Mental Illness by Thomas S. Szasz, M.D., © 1974, Harper & Row, Inc.

Society and the Healthy Homosexual by Dr. George Weinberg, © 1972 by George Weinberg, St. Martin's Press, Inc.

Gay American History: Lesbians & Gay Men in the U.S.A. by Jonathan Katz, © 1976, Thomas Y. Crowell.

Black Rage by William H. Grier, M.D., and Price M. Cobbs, M.D., © 1968 by William H. Grier and Price M. Cobbs, Basic Books, Inc., Publishers.

"The Development of an Identity: Power and Sex Roles in Academia," by Michael Silverstein in *The Journal of Applied Behavioral Science*, Volume 8, Number 5, © 1972, NTL Institute.

"I Could Move On" by Claudia Scott from *Lesbian Writer: Collected Work of Claudia Scott*, ed. by Frances Hanckel and Susan Windle, © 1981, Naiad Press.

Out of the Closets by Karla Jay and Allen Young, © 1972, Douglas Publishing.

Sappho Was a Right On Woman by Sidney Abbot and Barbara Love, © 1972, Stein & Day.

This Bridge Called My Back, edited by Cherríe Moraga and Gloria Anzaldúa, © 1981, Persephone Press, Inc. Reprinted by permission of the authors and publisher.

The Gay Report by Karla Jay and Allen Young, © 1979, Summit Books.

Gay Community News, August 22, 1981; May 23, 1981.

"14-Story Plunge From Skyscraper" by Michael Grieg, © 1980 *San Francisco Chronicle*. Reprinted by permission.

Lesbian/Woman by Del Martin and Phyllis Lyon, © 1972, Bantam Books.

Rat and the Devil: Journal Letters of F. O. Matthiessen and Russell Cheney, edited by Louis Hyde, © 1978, Archon Books.

On Lies, Secrets, and Silence by Adrienne Rich, © 1979, W. W. Norton & Co.

"I THOUGHT PEOPLE LIKE THAT
KILLED THEMSELVES"

1.

The Myth and the Fact
of Gay Suicide

There is nothing inherent in homosexual activity that would make a person self-destructive. Two human beings making love is a joyous thing, and infecting a type of love and sexual activity with hatred and violence is a terrible manipulation of the human experience. The power that society has had to coerce women who love women and men who love men into lives of degradation and humiliation is a true perversion of moral values.

Perhaps the most pernicious trick played on lesbians and gay men has been the creation of the dual myth of homosexual suicide. This myth asserts that lesbians and gay men not only commit suicide at a rate considerably higher than society-at-large but that somehow a person's homosexuality is itself the source of self-destructiveness. To understand how suicide and suicidal behavior became identified with lesbianism and male homosexuality in the public consciousness it is necessary to chart the development of societal attitudes towards both homosexuality and suicide. The two subjects, which share a parallel history of shame, ignorance and manipulation, became firmly linked only in the early part of the twentieth century when the emerging medical profession created a definition of the "homosexual personality" that included pathological behavior.

At various times throughout history both homosexual activity and suicide have been viewed more rationally than in our own time. Cultures that have been more accepting of homosexuality than our own have usually also held reasonable attitudes towards suicide. Classical Greece and Rome are examples of such cultures. Likewise, societies that have condemned the homosexual have held rigid taboos against suicide. The advent of Christianity in Western culture played a key role in making both homosexuality and suicide criminal acts.

Before the twentieth century, in America homosexuality and suicidal behavior were included in a long list of sinful acts willfully engaged in by "weak" persons. The concept of a woman or man who *was* homosexual and thus enjoyed same-sex sexual relations as a part of their nature was, as yet, virtually nonexistent. Hence persons "caught" in a homosexual act during this time were punished as "fallen" women and men—and considered to be sinners and criminals.

Lesbian and male homosexual activities have been outlawed in America since colonial days, and suicide and suicide attempts have been subject to legal penalties at various times throughout American history. Legal statutes banning these activities were imported to America by Europeans. The Puritans who settled in Massachusetts retained British attitudes towards sexuality which had become part of the canon of British law under Henry VIII.[1] The penalty for buggery was death. The Puritans also continued Christian Europe's attitudes towards suicide, which one writer has called "the history of official outrage and unofficial despair."[2]

Actual reports of executions of persons who engaged in homosexual activity are recorded in colonial America as early as 1646 when John Winthrop, the first governor of the Massachusetts Bay Colony, wrote in his *History of New England* about William Plaine of New Haven. Plaine "had committed sodomy with two persons in England, and that he had corrupted a great part of the youth of Guilford by masturbations, which he had committed, and provoked others to the like above a hundred times."[3]

During the same year, the *Calendar of Historical Manuscripts* recorded the execution of a black man, Jan Creoli, for a second offense of sodomy. Creoli was "choked to death" and "burnt to ashes."[4] Sexual activity between women was generally ignored by colonial courts, but at least one colony, New Haven, included lesbianism in its sodomy statute as a crime punishable by death.[5]

Public response to suicides and to people who had attempted suicide has been similar. In the Middle Ages, the body of the suicide was tortured and, if the victim was female, occasionally burned. In England, until the early nineteenth century, the corpse of the suicide was pierced with a stick and publicly dragged through the streets of the city. The victim's possessions were seized by the king. In Switzerland, the bodies of suicides were mutilated and, as in most Western European nations, buried in unconsecrated ground. In America, the New York State Penal Code in 1881 classified suicide as a crime, and attempted suicide was punishable by imprisonment and fine. Aiding or advising a person's suicide was considered the same as plotting a murder and is still a felony in many states.[6]

It was not until the publication of Emile Durkheim's *Le Suicide*, in 1897, that suicide was recognized not merely as the result of an individual's weak nature but as a response to social factors. Durkheim's work showed that, while some people were more vulnerable to suicidal actions than others (because their "mental constitution, as elaborated by nature and events, offers less resistance to the suicido-genetic current"[7]), the actual cause of suicide is related to social factors and especially to the integration of an individidual into society.

Similarly, while society of course realized that same-sex sexual activity was taking place during the many centuries of the historical past, the modern concepts of a lesbian woman and a homosexual man were not evolved until the late 1800s. Previously, homosexual acts, including sodomy, "women lying with women" and "men lying with men," were also viewed as isolated transgressions rather than as distinct and viable patterns of sexual behavior. The term "homosexuality" did not exist before 1869[8] and did not enter formal English until 1897 with the publication of Havelock Ellis' *Sexual Inversion*.[9] The concept was developed as a response to the growing awareness that same-sex sexual activity could be an integral part of a person's identity which was, in turn, brought on by a developing homosexual subculture in urban centers.

Thus it was that not until almost 1900 were either suicide or homosexuality seen as anything more than the actions of isolated individuals who had fallen victim to sin and crime. By this time, however, centuries of oppression had had their effect on lesbians and gay men. By considering homosexual activity to be a mortal sin, American culture forced countless women and men into lives of shame and desperation. It is clear to lesbian and gay male historians that many people involved in same-sex primary relationships did manage to live "careful" lives and appeared to have respectable "special" friendships.[10] Those people who were less fortunate and were "found out" had few options. One was to stand trial and accept the punishment. This option was chosen by many people charged with "lewd conduct," "sodomy" or under the "lying with" statutes. Many women and men were burnt at the stake, hung in public squares, castrated or beaten, while others were set free with a less harsh sentence. Another option was to flee, as Horatio Alger, author of many popular books for boys, chose to do in 1866 after he was charged with "the abominable and revolting crime of unnatural familiarity with boys" on Cape Cod.[11] A third option, taken by an untold number of women and men, was suicide.

In 1878, a corporal in the Seventh Cavalry stationed in the Dakota Territory killed himself after his partner, who had cross-dressed as a woman, died while the corporal was on a campaign. The cross-dressing was "discovered" when the man was laid out for his funeral. Don Rickey, Jr., in a study of the American West, reported, "The corporal's comrades ridiculed him unmercifully and, unable to bear their scorn, he committed suicide with his revolver."[12]

Sigmund Freud, writing around 1920, described the unhappy life of "a beautiful and clever girl of eighteen" who endured her parents' punishments and disapproval caused by her infatuation for an older woman. Freud describes this woman's suicide attempt:

> One day it happened, as, indeed, was sooner or later inevitable in the circumstances, that the father met his daughter in the company of the lady. He passed them by with an angry glance which boded no good. Immediately after the girl rushed off and flung herself over a neighboring wall on to the railway line. She paid for this undoubtedly serious attempt at suicide with a long stay in bed . . .[13]

While the examples cited by Freud and Rickey were obvious responses to public disapproval of homosexual relationships, it is not possible to determine the prevalence of this response. It is also impossible to assess the number of women and men who found their passions for their "friends" to be so intolerable that they cut their lives short, yet never acknowledged in any way their true feelings, thus placing themselves permanently outside the realm of lesbian and gay history. It does seem clear, however, that many lesbians and gay men throughout history have had to make the choice between public disgrace and suicide, and, unfortunately, many have chosen the latter.

"Respectable" people who lived satisfactory lives with same-sex partners were not usually suspected of engaging in homosexual practices. Female couples cohabiting in close familiar relationships in Boston in the nineteenth century were accepted as legitimate units in society and dubbed "Boston marriages."[14] These couples included Amy Lowell and Ada Russell, Sarah Orne Jewett and Annie Adams Fields, Katherine Lee Bates and Katherine Coman.[15] These relationships were not placed in league with those who engaged in same-sex sexual activity. Thus the only people whom the general public was aware of as enjoying homosexual activity were the victims—those women and men who were punished, executed, banished, or forced to flee or commit suicide. By observing only the victims, society came to see people engaging in homosexual activity as self-destructive. The victims defined this population.

By the mid-nineteenth century, when legal and medical writers began to study and classify same-sex sexual activity, homosexuality had already become linked to victimization. Since homosexuality had been seen earlier as an activity engaged in only by wicked people, it was easy to assume that their wickedness might take these people into other areas of crime. This assumption is most evident in the work of Western European writers who were the first to grapple with homosexuality as something more significant than spurious criminal activity.

The examination of same-sex sexual activity came about after the Industrial Revolution as urban centers grew and homosexual male subcultures developed in cities throughout Europe and America. As criminal codes were rewritten to regulate crimes in the growing industrial centers, homosexual acts were reexamined, along with other forms of nonprocreative sexuality, and categorized by medical "experts." Karl Heinrich Ulrichs, a homosexual German lawyer writing in the 1860s, was a pioneer in considering same-sex sexual activity as an inborn condition, and he developed a definition of what he named the "urning" or male homosexual and the "urningin" or lesbian.[16] According to Ulrichs, the urning and urningin were part of a third sex, born with the physical characteristics of one sex and the sexual and emotional responses of the other. Ulrichs' theories form the basis for the myth that lesbians are men trapped in women's bodies and that male homosexuals are women trapped in men's bodies.

Other "experts" studying homosexuality were also discovering that lesbians and gay men were, by nature, sick and violent. Richard von Krafft-Ebing authored a landmark volume of research into sex and sexuality and created categories for homosexuals: "sexual inversion as an acquired morbid phenomenon" and "sexual inversion as an innate morbid phenomenon." Krafft-Ebing quoted an anonymous British "man of high position" who stated:

I do not think I am far wrong when I maintain that at least half of the suicides of young men are due to this one circumstance. Even in cases where no merciless blackmailer persecutes the urning, but a connection has existed which lasted satisfactorily on both sides, still in these cases even discovery, or the dread of discovery, leads only too often to suicide. How many officers, who have had connection with their subordinates, how many soldiers, who have lived in such relation with a comrade, when they thought they were about to be discovered, have put a bullet through their brains to avoid the coming disgrace!"[17]

The writer continues, "mental abnormalities and real disturbances of the intellect are commoner with urnings than in the case of other men."

Albert Möll, the German author of *Die Konträre Sexual-empfindung* (1893), wrote that, "Many urnings come from nervous or pathologically disposed families" and that "when the love of a homosexual woman is not responded to, serious disturbances of the nerve-system may ensue, leading even to paroxysms of fury."[18] In 1886, Veniamin Tarnovsky, a leading Russian sexologist, wrote that homosexuals were born as the result of nervous disturbances of their parents, including epilepsy, brain disease, insanity, hysteria, alcoholism, syphilis, pneumonia, exhaustion or anemia.[19] Cesare Lombroso, the Italian author of a study of the criminal temperament, included homosexuals as a type of criminal suffering from a form of insanity that should be treated in asylums rather than prisons.[20]

Havelock Ellis' book *Sexual Inversion* (1897) has been called "the first book in English which·treated homosexuality as neither a disease nor a crime."[21] Yet, despite Ellis's attempts to make homosexuality or "inversion," as he called it, as normal as heterosexuality, he is also responsible for contributing to the stereotype of homosexuals, particularly of lesbians. Ellis wrote that female inversion was more common than male inversion and characterized female inverts as boyish, nervy, and having deep voices and the ability to whistle(!). Male inverts, for Ellis, resisted stereotyping, although they were prone to mild neurosis.

Perhaps the most detailed description of this characterization of the homosexual came from Edward Carpenter, a British socialist who wrote *The Intermediate Sex* (1908) and posited that homosexual women and men occupied an intermediate position between the male and female sex, an extension of Ulrichs' third sex theory. (A similar theory was put forward by Edward Stevenson in his book *The Intersexes* [1910].) Carpenter describes the "Uranian temperament" as a personality which mixes the male and the female. Himself homosexual (as was Stevenson), Carpenter writes: "with a good deal of experience in the matter, I think one may safely say that the defect of the male Uranian, or Urning, is *not* sensuality—but rather sentimentality."[22] He goes on to characterize male homosexuals as "gentle" and of an "emotional disposition." The male urning has "defects in the direction of subtlety, evasiveness, timidity, vanity etc.

while the female is just the opposite, fiery, active, bold and truthful, with defects running to brusqueness and coarseness." Carpenter's work, while eschewing the "disease" theories, is the strongest, most cohesive statement of a female and male homosexual *type* and contributed significantly to the establishment of stereotyped identities that were vulnerable to the manipulations of the medical profession. If lesbians and male homosexuals were "born that way," they should not be punished by the courts, they should be cured by doctors and psychiatrists. As homosexual activity moved from an isolated vice to an inborn condition, it moved in the public mind from a crime to an illness.

Once homosexuality was seen as an illness, the medical profession spent considerable energy analyzing its causes and searching for "the cure." The late nineteenth and early twentieth centuries saw an outpouring of literature by doctors, psychologists and sexologists in Germany, England, America and Italy on the subject of inversion. Since this was the only substantial literature available dealing with lesbians and homosexual males, the medical writer soon had full control of the public's understanding of homosexuality. The silence surrounding the real lives of lesbians and homosexual men again left a void to be filled by "experts" who based their understanding of "inversion" on people they interviewed in asylums, hospitals or prisons. The few lesbians and homosexual men who were writing on the subject often had difficulty getting their work published and distributed. Writing about books authored by doctors, John Addington Symonds noted that, "the phenomenon of sexual inversion is usually regarded in these books from the point of view of psychopathic or neuropathic derangement, inherited from morbid ancestors, and developed in the patient by early habits in self-abuse."[23]

Thus as male homosexuality and lesbianism were being defined for the first time as major aspects of a person's identity, psychological and emotional disorders were being integrated into the definition. Concurrently, the phenomenon of suicide was being reexamined and was evolving in a similar direction as homosexuality—away from being a sin or a crime and into being a sickness. As suicide shifted at the end of the nineteenth century from a moral issue to a medical issue, the writers searched for an understanding of the causes of suicide that came from outside rather than inside the individual. The work of Emile Durkheim contributed significantly to the view that social factors played a major role in causing suicides.

In *Le Suicide* (1897), Durkeim placed suicides into three categories:

egoistic suicide, which is suicide caused by a lack of integration of an individual into society; altruistic suicide, which is caused by an overabsorption of a person into society so that a life is sacrificed for a belief; and anomic suicide, which is brought on by a sudden drastic change in a person's social position. Durkheim examined groups of people who had higher suicide rates resulting from one of these factors. He asserted that married persons enjoy a certain degree of immunity to suicide, while unmarried persons are more susceptible. While he did not specifically look at a homosexual population, Durkheim clearly set the stage for later writers to fit "inverts" into the theory. Egoistic suicide appears to be the type of self-destruction to which the new homosexual population should be most vulnerable, since they were often on the fringes of society, or were integrated into a society in a manner that was based on undisclosed information or deliberate deception. Their integration was neither strong nor sincere, leaving them vulnerable to alienation and despair.[24] Durkheim provided a theory that the medical profession would soon develop into the myth of the suicidal homosexual.

And the medical profession has continued to develop and refine the myth of the suicidal homosexual throughout the twentieth century, embellishing lesbian and gay male identities with quirks to fit the latest psychoanalytic theory. Occasionally a bit of insight has been injected into the discussion of homosexuality and suicide by a particularly sensitive doctor, as in the case of Dr. Max Marcuse's article "Suicide and Sexuality," published in the *Journal of Sexology and Psychanalysis*, in 1923:

> According to Hirschfeld's estimate, the incidence of suicides owing to homosexuality is about 3 percent, of all urnings, and of the suicides directly due to homosexuality he distinguishes, besides those due to worry over their abnormality, three subdivisions, namely, (1) those committed during criminal proceedings against the respective homosexual individual; (2) those caused by blackmail; (3) those connected with a threatening scandal. Homosexuality may be the *indirect* cause of suicide where not the homosexual predisposition itself leads to the catastrophe, but where the homosexual inclinations have thrown the victim into situations with which he is unable to cope. In a considerable number of "shocking individual fatalities," the consciousness of the standards of society, and, finally, the suicide, follow one another in an uncannily monotonous sequence.[25]

More typical are the comments of W. A. O'Connor, writing in the *British Journal of Medical Psychology* in 1948. In an article titled,

"Some Notes on Suicide," O'Connor equates homosexual desire with a warped sexual identity and thus engages in the common medical tactic of stigmatizing the homosexual:

> More than 50% of the material here presented uncovered the factor of homosexual tendencies. This may be accidental, and no statistical value is claimed for it, striking though it be. Taking the libidinal development as a whole, however, and without laying special emphasis on positive homosexual findings, we are faced with the question, touched upon at the beginning of this paper: in practically every case, that is in more than 90% of the material, the sexual life was unsatisfactory to a marked degree, either in the direction of weakness of the heterosexual urge or of strength of the homosexual urge, or both.[26]

The most dangerous assertions that the medical profession has been responsible for have been attempts to see homosexuality as inherently self-destructive and to probe the psyches of lesbians and gay men for the root motivation that causes their "illness":

> The homosexual act in itself may already represent a suicidal tendency, an inner fury against prolonging the race, or an unconscious need to merge with the stronger person of the same sex.[27]

The ability of a small group of doctors, lawyers, criminologists and sexologists to forge what became known as the "homosexual type," and to infuse this type with self-destructive tendencies, is best understood by realizing that they had control over the limited sources of information concerning lesbians and male homosexuals. Until the early twentieth century, popular literature and the press were silent about the lives of homosexuals. Since homosexuals themselves were gagged by societal condemnation, the small group of "experts" monopolized the market. In the same way that women in Western culture have been defined by men, and white people have defined people of color, primarily heterosexual writers and publishers defined female and male homosexuals. `

Most Americans certainly never read these articles or books, yet the theories they put forward strongly influenced the public's understanding of lesbians and gay men. Jeannette Foster wrote, "By 1900 most of these men's [Krafft-Ebing, Möll, Hirschfeld, Symonds, Ellis, Carpenter] contributions to the subject were in print and widely disseminated, so that in scientific and intellectual circles there was much talk of an intermediate sex whose condition was referred to as *inversion.*"[28]

If medical and legal literature provided the germ for the "homosexuality is sickness" theory, popular literature, plays, novels, films and magazine articles infected public attitudes with this message. From the early part of this century to the present, the media has molded the theories of the "experts" into "real-life" situations and created an image of the homosexual as sick, miserable and desperate. As homosexual women and men have been studied and categorized by doctors, psychoanalysts, and psychiatrists, popular literature, movies and plays have reflected the findings and brought their message to the general public.

The effect this has had on the linkage of homosexuality and suicide becomes apparent in surveying lesbian literature. Jeannette Foster's study of the lesbian in Western literature, *Sex Variant Women in Literature*, contains reference after reference to suicidal lesbian characters.[29] Beginning with what Foster terms Sappho's purely "legendary" suicide [see Appendix 1], the book guides the reader through centuries of self-destructive lesbians. Foster makes it clear that the pages of literature about lesbians are filled with schoolgirls who leap out of windows because of crushes on their schoolmistresses, women who slit their wrists because their women lovers forsake them for men (the *real* thing), lesbians who blow their brains out after they are publicly exposed, "heterosexual" women who turn on the gas after being seduced by depraved lesbians, and self-hating dykes who drink themselves to death in lonely, sleazy bars. In a section on nineteenth-century literature, Foster writes:

> Of the more than a dozen authors who took overt lesbianism as a major theme, seven . . . condemned it explicitly, though with differing degrees of severity. Seven others . . . made lesbian affairs responsible for murder, suicide and ruin, and so implied equally strong condemnation.[30]

When Foster reviews European fiction during the first half of the twentieth century, she finds no change:

> One feature of these foreign twentieth-century novels which must strike even a casual observer is the high incidence of suicide among variant women. Physical or mental illness is also often attributed to lesbian practices. Both reflect the extent to which variant fiction was based on clinical reading.[31]

Other writers have noted the preponderance of self-destructive lesbians and gay men in literature and film. Ann Aldrich, in her book *We Two Won't Last* (1963), wrote,

> Though there have been, in this country, four motion pictures

shown with lesbianism as the theme (*Mädchen in Uniform, Pit of Loneliness, Olivia* and *The Children's Hour*), all four involved the suicide of a principal character.[32]

Vito Russo conveniently (for this writer) includes a "Necrology" in his book *The Celluloid Closet: Homosexuality in the Movies.* In the appendix he lists over a dozen suicides and almost two dozen murders of homosexual characters.[33] Likewise, Donald Webster Cory observed in 1951 that male homosexual literature is rife with self-destruction:

> Another fiction: the homosexual is a depressed, dejected person, frequently on the brink of suicide, or actually ending his hopeless life after many years of despondent struggle. This portrait is probably further from the truth than any other, and to some extent its wide acceptance may be attributed to the novelists who have ended so many books on this subject in the mood of despair, violence, and even suicide. *The City and the Pillar, The Fall of Valor, The Sling and the Arrow, The Invisible Glass, Stranger in the Land, Special Friendships, Twilight Men,* and *Finistère*—among many others—all end with hopelessness for the invert. Several of these books bring the invert to self-destruction; the others leave him no other path to follow.[34]

It is not difficult for anyone familiar with gay literature to name dozens of novels and stories that climax with the suicide of a homosexual. What is even more disconcerting, however, is the realization that in the thirty years since Cory wrote this statement, there has been little change in the attitude towards lesbians and gay men in literature and the media. *Time* magazine, in an early piece on gay people in 1969, quoted Mart Crowley, the author of *The Boys in the Band.* "Homosexuality used to be a sensational gimmick," Crowley says. "The big revelation in the third act was that the guy was homosexual, and then he had to go offstage and blow his brains out. It was associated with sin, and there had to be retribution."[35]

While *Time* and Crowley seem to agree that times have changed, a study of literature since the development of the lesbian and gay movements shows that change is slow to come. *The Boys in the Band,* often considered to be a landmark play in dealing with male homosexual themes, gave us the line, "Show me a happy homosexual and I'll show you a gay corpse."[36] Novels continue to be filled with suicide and victimization, including *Fortune and Men's Eyes, Dancer from the Dance, The Sergeant, Giovanni's Room, Happy Endings All Alike, Good Times, Bad Times, Trying Hard to Hear You, The Front Runner,* and *Cruising.* In addition to novels with specifically gay themes, popular books that include a gay character who ends up killing herself or himself continue to flood the market. Movies that need to find motivation for a character's unhappiness or suicide, throw in a gay incident, such as occurred in *Ode to Billy Joe*. The only major changes that have taken place in the literature over the past ten years have been the development of healthy lesbian and, to a lesser extent, gay male characters in novels written by gay people themselves and usually published by small presses and the slow shift from suicidal behavior on the part of gay characters to violent acts directed at them from outside sources.

Literature focused on homosexuals prior to the 1960s was primarily pulp fiction and medical literature, although more recently a change has occurred and journalists have given wider coverage to lesbians and gay men. Magazine editors generally considered to be urbane and "liberal" applauded themselves on covering a controversial minority with sensitivity, while journalistic forays into the worlds of lesbians and gay men have reeked of exploitation and stereotyping. Consider a *Harper's Magazine* piece from 1963 titled "New York's Middle-Class Homosexuals," written by William J. Helmer:

> The homosexual's position in society is often precarious. Discovery can cost him his reputation and perhaps his career. He is aware that, according to New York law, every sexual act could cost him years in prison (though it rarely happens). He feels society hates him, and unjustly. Frequently he is guilt-ridden, aware or not, and lacks the self-acceptance he needs in order to live comfortably with his condition, which itself is thought to be closely related to an unhealthy early psychological environment. These factors, rather than homosexuality alone, are what some believe to be the main causes of emotional instability, effeminism, violence, and other problems commonly blamed on sexual deviation.[37]

Or, more recently, a 1972 *Saturday Review* article, "Homosex: Living the Life" by Faubion Bowers:

> There are, indeed, terribly sad aspects of homosexuality, and to suggest otherwise is deceitful. For instance, three homosexuals committed suicide during Gay Pride Week in New York in 1971. The gay liberationists cry "Change society!" accenting the positive in order to eliminate the negative. The psychiatrists say, "Change the symptoms." But as matters stand in this lifetime, both cause and effect must change. I have had occasion to know homosexuals who tell me they can never escape their reverberating nimbus of guilt, who liken their nights of loveless sex to daggers of icicles,

who remind themselves hourly of their futility as men . . .I know a
fifty-year-old homosexual who, not having found a stationary
kind of affection in his life, has contemplated death, and some
younger ones who have actually tried it. I know, further, homosexuals whose bitterness against the world is so blindly diffuse that
they try to destroy everyone around them.[38]

Articles in the mainstream press almost invariably include a look
at miserable, suicidal men and women. The inclusion of the unhappy serves as both a threat and a deterrent to the closeted homosexual reader: coming out may lead to a life of desperation. To write
about suicidal homosexuals without connecting self-destructive tendencies to the oppression which is its root cause is to again blame the
victim for the crime visited upon her or him. This is, more recently,
a major feature of the Right's political campaign against lesbians and
gay men. [See Appendix 2]

It is difficult to prove that popular literature's depiction of lesbians and gay men as suicidal actually influences an individual's
suicidal feelings. The free and open discussion of suicide has histori-
cally been challenged by individuals who believe that such discussion
will impel people to commit suicide. As early as 1845, doctors were
recommending that newspapers omit information about suicides:

> That suicides are alarmingly frequent in this country is evident to
> all—and as a means of prevention, we respectfully suggest the
> propriety of not publishing the details of such occurrences. "No
> fact," says a late writer, "is better established in science than that
> suicide is often committed from imitation. A single paragraph
> may suggest suicide to 20 persons. Some particulars of the act, or
> expressions, seize the imagination, and the disposition to repeat it,
> in a moment of morbid excitement, proves irresistible." In the
> justness of these remarks we concur, and commend them to the
> consideration of the conductors of the periodical press.[39]

Studies have shown, however, that newspaper reportage of suicidal behavior does not appear to increase the incidence of suicides.[40]
What is not clear is the possible effect of the assumption that homosexuals are suicidal on the early identity formation of lesbians and
gay men. Growing into the awareness that one is homosexual and
into the identity of a lesbian or gay man, without knowing others like
oneself, leaves a person susceptible to whatever information they
come across concerning homosexuals. If that information is rife with
assumptions of sickness, self-destructiveness and inner conflict, it is
entirely possible for the gay person's self-concept to suffer irrepara-
bly. As George Weinberg has written:

The homosexual is not told like the black that he is stupid. He is not told like the Jew that he is mercenary. The almost invariable expression of disdain for homosexuals is that they are neurotic, "sick"—that the homosexual has a malformed psyche. Many homosexuals have accepted this as true, and suffer because of a bias held against themselves.[41]

While it is true that many homosexuals suffer because society stereotypes them as unhappy, unhealthy individuals, the extent of that suffering is difficult to determine. Although some studies indicate that the expectations specific professions place on certain populations play a major role in shaping the identities of those populations, such studies are limited and cannot necessarily be applied to the expectations that society has for lesbians and gay men. Have lesbians and gay men internalized the myths of homosexuals as suicidal and engaged in massive self-destruction?

Lesbians and gay men have had to confront the myths of gay suicide and deny or acknowledge their validity. Donald Webster Cory wrote, in 1951: "Few suicides are homosexuals and few homosexuals commit suicide. Perhaps homosexuals are so accustomed to the slings and the arrows of a life in which they have been buffeted from one difficulty to another that they find it easy to accept a philosophical approach to the torments of human existence."[42]

A decade later, Ann Aldrich wrote, "As a practicing lesbian of many years, with wide acquaintanceship of many homosexuals, both male and female, I have not found suicide or suicidal tendencies at all particular to homosexuals. I will not say that I have not known of homosexuals who have taken their lives, or made attempts on their lives, but as little as I have been familiar with these cases, I have also known as many who were not homosexuals."[43]

For many years, homosexual writers have denied the myth that homosexuals are more susceptible to suicide. The denial took place in the same context in which the myths were created: without statistics, without a view of the entire lesbian and male homosexual population, and with little awareness of the difficulties in defining or verifying suicides. In recent years, however, more and more writers have acknowledged the existence of suicide in the community. Del Martin and Phyllis Lyon provided some startling information in *Lesbian/Woman* (1972):

Del contemplated suicide; others have attempted it, and some have succeeded. Because of our own experience we are keenly aware of the identity crisis every Lesbian must face: that period in her life when she is forced to come to terms with the reality that she is at odds with the society in which she lives. We have known that thoughts of suicide often occur to the young woman, like Del, who cannot reconcile her actual feelings with those expected of her by her family, by her religion, or by her peers. But we had no idea how prevalent suicide is until we learned of a recent (1971) discussion involving twenty Lesbians between the ages of twenty-five and thirty-two, where it was revealed that only two had not attempted suicide when they were teenagers. It was shocking to us that eighteen out of twenty young women had been made to feel so degraded by the realization of their Lesbian identity, their self image so debased, that suicide seemed to be their only out.[44]

Within the past five years studies have provided the statistical information needed to determine whether lesbians and gay men are in reality suicidal risk groups. Since most of the statistics were gathered during the 1970s, it is important to acknowledge the limitations of such data. Changing attitudes toward lesbianism and male homosexuality, along with the increased visibility of lesbians and gay men, are radically transforming the self-concepts of gay people. Lesbians and gay men discovering their sexual identities in the 1980s have more options regarding life decisions than gay people in the 1970s. Today we realize that because of the changing status of the lesbian and the male homosexual, studies done during a certain period of time may not be fully pertinent a decade later. This factor is magnified because most of the lesbians and gay men in the studies experienced the formative stages in the development of their self-images during a time when healthy models of gay people were unavailable. Many people believe that young women and men growing up today will have healthier attitudes towards their sexuality and their identity as lesbians and gay men than gay people before the changes brought about by the lesbian, gay male and feminist movements.

The studies are further hampered because the two factors we are attempting to isolate—homosexuality and suicide—are both difficult to assess in a population. None of the studies cited below claims to have surveyed a representative cross section of lesbians and gay men. An attempt to define specifically who is included in such a study would lead to many difficult questions. Does one include only those people who can publicly or privately identify themselves as lesbians or gay men? Is a woman included if she engages in sexual activity with other women yet defines herself as heterosexual? Where do bisexuals fit into the study? While each of the directors of the studies had to attempt to answer these questions, none was able to obtain responses from all segments of the population, and the studies must be looked at with this limitation in mind.

Assessing the rate of attempted and completed suicide in any population is also difficult. Suicide still carries a stigma of shame, inadequacy and failure, and many people who have attempted to take their lives or have seriously considered suicidal actions subsequently deny that they have. Families often discourage coroners from listing a relative's death as suicide because of familial pride. In addition to the personal factors involved in the reporting of suicides and suicide attempts, death certification in the United States is a function of the states rather than the federal government. States have different systems for the certification of death and have differing legal definitions of suicide. Automobile accidents—thought by some suicidologists to be a major method of suicide—are frequently listed in a different category or under the general heading "accidents," rather than considered on a case-by-case basis and occasionally included as suicides. Some coroners require a suicide note before they will classify a death as a suicide, although a study done of reported suicides in Los Angeles indicated that only 35% of the suicides actually left notes.[45] A study of the certification procedure of suicide in eleven Western states led researchers to conclude that their work "calls into question the validity and comparability of reported suicide rates."[46]

Deaths occurring through many methods traditionally thought to be accidents—including drug overdoses and falls from high places—are usually never listed as suicides. Chronic self-destructive behavior, through alcoholism, for example, may result in self-inflicted death; but because the death is not immediate and not violent, it is not considered as suicide. Many psychiatrists and suicidologists are now looking at this form of self-destructive behavior and studying its relationship to suicide. Because of all of these factors, any statistics on suicide are thought to be well below the actual figures.

Most of the studies of gay people and suicide are studies of living people and are therefore studies of suicide attempts rather than completed suicides. There is a complex relationship between suicide attempts and actual completed suicides. What an individual might intend to be a suicide attempt, a cry for help, can become a completed suicide if that person does not realize the dosage of pills taken is unsafe. In considering these studies, we can only say that the number of suicide attempts is estimated at six to ten times the number of completed suicides.[47] There seems to be little correlation between attempted and completed suicides in certain populations. For example, women seem to comprise over 70% of the suicide attempts in the United States, but less than 30% of the completed suicides.[48]

While these considerations call into question the accuracy of the statistics for suicides and attempted suicides and the representative nature of the lesbian and gay male population studies, they do form a body of recent information which will aid us in arriving at some general conclusions.

BELL & WEINBERG STUDY

In 1970, Alan Bell and Martin Weinberg, of Indiana University's Institute for Sex Research, conducted a study of lesbians and gay men in the San Francisco area.[49] The team hired homosexuals specifically for the purpose of locating and recruiting participants for their comprehensive research during the summer and fall of 1969. They located potential participants through public advertising, bars, personal contacts, baths, lesbian and gay male organizations, mailing lists, and meetings in public areas. Over 5,000 potential participants were recruited and Bell and Weinberg selected their final sample from this pool, mindful of the participant's recruitment source, age, educational level, sex and race. Their final sample included 575 white homosexual men, 111 black homosexual men, 229 white lesbians and 64 black lesbians.

Bell and Weinberg state emphatically in their introduction that "any consensus about the exact number of homosexual men or women exhibiting this or that characteristic is not an aim of the present study. The nonrepresentative nature of other investigators' samples as well as our own precludes any generalization about the incidence of a particular phenomenon even to persons living in the locale where the interviews were conducted, much less homosexuals in general. Nowhere has a random sample of American homosexual men and women ever been obtained."[50] While their study is certainly of great significance, it clearly does not contain a large enough sample of either blacks and other people of color or lesbians to be used reliably as a determinant for their behavior.

Bell and Weinberg also chose heterosexual respondent group members using probability sampling with quotas and thus the heterosexuals were chosen to match the homosexual respondents in terms of race, sex, age and education. The heterosexual study group consisted of 284 white men, 53 black men, 101 white women, and 39 black women.

Regarding suicide, Bell and Weinberg found that 37% of the white homosexual men had either seriously considered or attempted suicide, compared to 13% of the white heterosexual men; of the black homosexual men 24% had seriously considered or attempted suicide, compared to 2% of the black heterosexual men. Of the white lesbians 41% had similar experiences, compared to 26% of the white heterosexual women; and 25% of the black lesbians had seriously considered or attempted suicide, compared with 19% of the black heterosexual women.

When asked, "What were the reasons you tried it [suicide] the first time?", slightly over half of those gay respondents who had ever attempted suicide stated that it was caused by "distress not related to homosexuality." The other half strongly stated that their attempts were related to difficulty with sociosexual homosexual adjustment, or dealing with the external world. A small, but significant, percentage of those lesbians and gay men who had attempted suicide attributed the first attempt to "acceptance of one's homosexuality" or the internal acceptance of being gay (16% of the white homosexual men, 9% of the black homosexual men, 4% of the white lesbians, and 9% of the black lesbians). When those lesbians and gay men who considered suicide were asked for their reasons, statistics similar to those who had actually attempted suicide appear.

Despite Bell and Weinberg's insistence that their study not be used to determine the percentage of lesbians or gay men exhibiting any specific characteristic or behavior, it does allow them to conclude that: "The homosexual men tended to feel less self-accepting and more lonely, depressed, and tense than did the heterosexual men . . . They were much more likely to have considered or attempted suicide, although, according to the respondents, this was not necessarily connected to their homosexuality." The black gay men "tended to be less likely ever to have considered suicide" than the white homosexual men, though more likely than heterosexual black men. Lesbians reported more "suicidal ideation" than their heterosexual counterparts, and, again, white lesbians reported more likelihood to consider or attempt suicide than black lesbians.[51]

SAGHIR & ROBINS STUDY

In 1973, Marcel Saghir and Eli Robins published *Male and Female Homosexuality: A Comprehensive Investigation.*[52] Their study compared a sample of homosexual women and men from Chicago and San Francisco with a sample of unmarried heterosexuals drawn from a "singles" apartment complex in St. Louis County. Their sample of lesbians and gay men was drawn largely from early gay organizations including the Daughters of Bilitis, the Mattachine Society, *One* magazine, and the Society for Individual Rights. They studied only white women and men, and the sample included 89 homosexual men, 57 lesbians, 40 heterosexual men, and 44 heterosexual women. The study is primarily of middle-class and upper-middle-class people.

Saghir and Robins found that 7% of the homosexual men had attempted suicide while none of their heterosexual male sample had; 12% of the lesbians had attempted suicide while only 5% of the heterosexual women had. The homosexual men had primarily made their attempts before they reached the age of 20, or, as the authors stated, "during the latter part of adolescent years, when conflict at home and with one's self concerning homosexuality was intense." The suicide attempts by the young men often involved a frustrated relationship or an argument with parents, and Saghir and Robins concluded that: "Usually the suicide attempt was directly or indirectly related to homosexuality." They also noted that "Suicide attempts among the homosexual women tended to be somewhat more serious than among homosexual men."

In a preliminary study for their book, Saghir and Robins, along with Bonnie Walbran and Kathye A. Gentry, noted:

A substantial proportion (23 percent) of homosexual women attempt suicide. While the incidence of suicide in homosexuals is not known, the significance of suicide attempts in general and their relationship to completed suicide has been well documented. It is estimated that the incidence of subsequent suicide among persons making suicidal attempts is between ten and 20 percent. Furthermore, homosexual women have a high prevalence of alcohol abuse and depression. These conditions have been shown to be directly related to an increased risk of mortality from suicide. Consequently, this triad of suicide attempts, affective disorders, and alcohol abuse should be of primary consideration whenever a homosexual woman seeks out psychiatric help. Hospitalization might be the necessary initial step during an acute crisis situation.[53]

JAY & YOUNG STUDY

Perhaps the most extensive and comprehensive study of lesbians and gay men so far is *The Gay Report*, a study done in 1977 (and released in 1979) of over 5,000 lesbians and gay men, ranging in age from 14 to 82 and living in the United States and Canada.[54] The

respondents to the questionnaire which the authors drafted included gay people from every state in the United States and every
province in Canada. They lived in rural areas and suburbs as well as
in cities of all sizes. The sample group was over 90% white, with only
1% of the lesbians and 2% of the gay men respondents being black
people. Fewer than 1% of the respondents were Asian American or
Native American, and only 1.6% of the women and 1% of the men
were Hispanic. The final study included 4,400 gay men and 1,000
lesbians.

The study was conducted through questionnaires publicized in
the gay press or occasionally printed in their entirety in several
newspapers and journals. The questionnaires were also distributed
to lesbians and gay men who had placed personal ads in classified
sections of newspapers, at bars and businesses, at organizations and
social events. The two twelve-page questionnaires, one for women
and one for men, consisted of both short answer and essay questions
where respondents could explain their experiences and thoughts
more fully.

Both lesbians and gay men were asked the questions "Have you
ever attempted or seriously contemplated suicide?" and "If yes, was
this experience related to your lesbianism (or homosexuality)?" In
addition, women and men were asked to "Please tell us something
about the following topics. If you have strong feelings about them,
or any interesting experiences, please share them with us." Letter "j"
on the list was "suicide."

In response to the statistical questions, 40% of the men and 39%
of the women stated that they had attempted or seriously contemplated suicide. 53% of the men and 33% of the women who had
considered or attempted suicide said that their homosexuality was a
factor.

The essay question responses contained some fascinating quotations:

"During my first years of coming out I considered suicide often
enough not to be frightened by it. I knew how I would do it. There
were times that acknowledging my homosexuality was so painful
that suicide seemed an alternative. No more; I want to live and I
want to live gay."

"I thought about it a lot when I was an adolescent dyke and
sometimes really wanted to do it because I thought my being here
was all a big mistake. But then I realized *that's* what all the straight

people wanted—for us misfits to just quietly off ourselves. So I decided to teach them a lesson and go on living. Besides, I was scared to do it. That was good judgment on my part and I'm glad I'm still here. I don't ever give it more than a second thought, and am no longer 'half in love with easeful death.' (I memorized Keats' 'Nightingale' when I was 17, and to remember it still makes me tremble and cry and think about a handful of white pills. That's an association I'd like to lose, but I'm afraid it will be with me always!)"

"I have lived in total fear of my company, friends, or family learning of my homosexuality. I have lived with complete guilt related to my actions. In late 1973 I attempted suicide by drowning. I did not have the guts to keep my head below water, but learned that I am a strong endurance swimmer. Fortified with brandy, I started swimming straight out at 2:00 a.m. When the sun came up I was still far enough out that I could not see 40-story buildings on the coast. I got back at 8:00 a.m. and spent two weeks in a psychiatric ward."

"I shall indeed resort to suicide as soon as my father dies. (To do so while he is alive would be to saddle him with a great sorrow.) I think *any* gay over age 45 or 50 should kill himself, as he has almost no chance of sex, aside from buying it from male prostitutes." .

"I believe that there are cases when suicide is a person's sanest and most responsible choice; these suicides are usually well planned and always successful. However, suicide attempts which fail and fail repeatedly are either desperate cries for help, or techniques for manipulating and punishing others; in both cases some sort of crisis-intervention help is probably appropriate. I believe, as my therapist friends all claim, that probably 80-90% of all suicide attempts have some gay-related element to them; in other words, suicide is one manifestation of homophobic social values. But successful suicides are rarely due to gayness itself but other and permanent problems."[55]

It is significant, however, that Jay and Young conclude: "There is no doubt that suicide and attempted suicide are frequent responses of gay people to the difficulties of the gay experience in a hostile society. It has been suggested that psychiatrists, clergy, and others who insist on characterizing gays as sick and sinful are responsible for driving many gay people to suicide. It is a form of violent oppression resulting from isolation, discrimination, and the problems of survival."

STUDIES OF MARITAL STATUS

Additional clues to the suicide risk for lesbians and gay men may be found in statistics on suicide and marital status. Studies have shown that most lesbians and gay men are either single or divorced. The Bell & Weinberg study indicated that 20% of the gay men had been married at some time in their lives or were currently married and 35% of the white lesbians and 47% of the black lesbians were of similar status.[56] The Jay and Young report found that 7% of the gay men were currently married, 2% were separated from their wives, 9% were divorced and 82% were single.[57] Although Jay and Young provide no statistics on separations and divorce among lesbians, their study does show that only 7% of the lesbians surveyed were currently married.[58]

By looking at the statistics for suicide by marital status, it is clear that single people and divorced people are at greater risk for suicide than married people. United States government statistics for 1970 indicate that single and divorced people have a higher suicide rate than married people. For some age ranges, there is a significant difference between the rates. For example, for people between the ages of 25 and 34, the suicide rate for single people is double the rate for married people. The rate for divorced people is considerably higher.[59]

Additional studies support this data. An article in the *Journal of Health and Social Behavior* reported that single women between the ages of 25 and 64 are 47% more likely to commit suicide than married women in the same age bracket. The same study showed that single men are 97% more likely to commit suicide than married men.[60] *California Medicine* reported that "suicide is more frequent in the single than the married"[61] and an article in *Lancet* showed that, while only 6% of the British population lived alone, over 22% of the people who completed suicides lived alone.[62] At a symposium on suicide at George Washington University's School of Medicine in 1965, Dr. Stanley Yolles stated, "We know that the marital status of an individual has a definite relationship to potential suicide risk, and national statistics bear this out. For single persons, the rate is 20.9 (33.2 for males and 7.7 for females), for married persons, 11.9."[63]

While one recent study[64] indicates that the statistics on marital status and suicide may be changing, it appears that currently unmarried people—single, divorced, separated, widowed—are at greater risk for suicide than married people. Since most lesbians and gay men are not married, these statistics provide additional data that supports the previous studies' conclusions that place gay people at higher risk for suicide than heterosexuals.

MISCELLANEOUS STUDIES

In 1977, the *Journal of Nervous and Mental Disease* published a study of 95 women prisoners from the Framingham Institution for Women in Massachusetts, a correctional facility. In evaluating the data accumulated, the team divided the women into three groups: women who were self-identified as lesbians, women who were self-identified as nonhomosexuals, and women who did not identify themselves as lesbians but were considered to be homosexual by the institution's staff. The arbitrary nature of permitting an institution's staff to define prisoners as lesbian or as heterosexual is a factor which qualifies significantly the results of this study. The authors of the study concluded that "the self-reported homosexual women reported significantly more suicide thoughts, suicide attempts . . . than did non-homosexuals."[65]

Another study of 25 young lesbians between the ages of 12 and 17 in a junior-senior high school in New York City who were referred to psychiatrists for psychiatric evaluation surprised reseachers Malvina Kremer and Alfred Rifkin with the high rate of incidents of suicide attempts. They wrote, "Two had made suicide attempts and one had threatened suicide. Surprisingly, nine others were found to have depressive episodes and five had made suicidal gestures or attempts of some sort."[66]

All these studies share several serious flaws: failure to obtain a representative group of lesbians and gay men, limited inclusion of people of color, and the inability to definitively correlate suicide attempts with completed suicides. These concerns seriously qualify the findings of the studies and make necessarily general any conclusions derived from them.

It is, however, possible to draw two conclusions from this accumulated data: 1. Lesbians are a significantly higher risk population for suicide than heterosexual women; 2. Gay men are a significantly higher risk population for suicide than heterosexual men. While these conclusions validate the thesis that lesbians and gay men are higher risk groups for suicide than the heterosexual population, it is important to note again that this thesis was originally created over many years with no statistical information as basis. Whether lesbians and gay men were a high risk population at that time, or whether the suicidal tendencies of the only visible gay people helped define the entire gay population as suicidal, we will never know for certain.

It is important to note also what we cannot conclude from these studies. We cannot adequately estimate how much greater the risk of suicide is for gay people. We cannot conclude that homosexuality or lesbianism causes suicide or that suicidal people are "vulnerable" to homosexuality. And, because we only have recent statistics, we cannot determine if the suicide rate for lesbians and gay men is currently increasing or decreasing.

To answer the questions that remain about lesbians, gay men and suicide, further studies will have to be done. It is my hope that conductors of studies of suicide—suicidologists and psychiatrists, epidemiologists and sociologists—will realize the importance of considering sexual orientation as an important variable to assess.

It is also my hope that the conclusions reached in this book will motivate lesbians and gay men to more aggressive work in the area of suicide prevention. While lesbian and gay male activists have understandably remained aloof from the issue of suicide in the gay population, properly fearing that antigay forces would use the statistics as ammunition for their "gay-is-sick" campaigns (as they have done), these studies indicate that lesbians and gay men need to arrive at a broader understanding of the issues concerning suicide in the gay population. The lesbian and gay male communities, as well as suicide prevention workers and other health professionals, need to grow into a greater awareness of the special risk factors within the gay population as well as the political issues that underlie the suicides of every lesbian and gay man.

Blackmail
Exposure

*oing to get a suicide out of this."—Rev. Roy Birchard of
*itan Community Church after more than 100 men were
arrested a~.. *ed with solicitation in St. Louis' Tower Grove Park
during the summer of 1979, as quoted in* The Advocate *(October, 1979).*

As long as lesbianism and male homosexuality are considered sick,
sinful or criminal by society-at-large, women and men who lead lives
which include sexual involvement with others of their sex will weigh
cautiously the risks and benefits resulting from being open about
their sexual orientation. Publicly identifying oneself as a lesbian or
gay man is a relatively new option for gay people and one which is
still outside the realm of practical possibility for most. Prior to the
development of the gay movement, public identification as a homosexual was, almost by definition, linked to scandal, social ostracism,
blackmail and suicide.

To think that the days of blackmail and suicide are over for gay
people is a naive assumption resulting from an ignorance of contemporary life. Most gay people are as vulnerable to exposure as
ever. In fact, perhaps since more people are aware of lesbianism and
male homosexuality today than twenty years ago, gay people who
attempt to "pass" as heterosexual have a greater risk of discovery
than in the past. Although the political gay movement has not
resulted in the elimination of suicides resulting from public exposure, it has provided a model and an option that may be chosen by
lesbians and gay men whose homosexuality has been revealed. Prior
to the past twenty years, exposed gay people tended to either deny
their true sexuality or risk reactions that were often devastating.
Today, many gay people can choose to "go public" and face substantially less horror. This is not to say that contemporary lesbians and
gay men always choose this option; they often do not. The mere
existence of the option, however, has given lesbians and gay men an
alternative to either total disgrace or total denial.

Suicides brought about by exposure as a result of police action are in a distinct category of gay suicide which primarily involves gay men. These suicides occur when a man has been entrapped by a police officer, observed engaging in sexual activities in a public place, or accused of engaging in same-sex sexual activity by another. In 1914, a male homosexual scholar from Colorado wrote: "Four years ago there was an engineering student here who was carrying on with boys in the YMCA building; he was arrested and taken to the police station, where he killed himself with a revolver. He was the son of a professor."[1]

These arrests, commonly cited for "morals charges," have traditionally been tantamount to public disgrace, family shame, and the devastation of one's career.

In recent years, many gay activists have targeted police entrapment of gay men in cruising areas as a practice which creates a "victimless crime" and wastes taxpayers' money. Despite public demands that more police be assigned to preventing violent crimes and fewer police to the patrol of cruising areas, entrapment and vice squad arrests on "morals charges" continue to intrude into the lives of gay men in many communities.

Those arrested on these charges are often men who are not a part of the politically active gay community. They may be men who are unable, for many reasons, to enter into the gay community in other ways. They may be married men who cannot afford to be seen in a gay bar, or they may be young men who do not identify this kind of sexual encounter as homosexual. One group of men who have been particularly vulnerable to arrests on "morals charges" are boy-lovers, who continue to be subject to tremendous harassment and legal prosecution. While there are certainly many openly gay men who frequent public parks and rest areas for sexual encounters, large numbers of the men who find themselves facing police officers on vice charges are neither aware of their rights nor comfortable enough with their sexuality to avoid panic.

Suicides brought on as a result of police entrapment often appear as tragic stories sensationalized in newspapers. A survey of the Los Angeles area press of the early 1950s reveals dozens of accounts of these morals cases.[2] The *Los Angeles Herald Express* of June 30, 1951, reported the death of psychiatrist Dr. William Peake in a story headlined, "Accused Physician Ends Life: Beach Psychiatrist in Morals Case Takes Sleep Pills." Dr. Peake had been arrested on four charges involving sexual activities with teenage boys. At the time of his arrest, he told the officers, in the words of the newspaper, "he had had unnatural tendencies since early boyhood" and that he was aware that "a cure of homosexuality is not possible." After writing a farewell note to his wife and daughter, Peake went to a hotel room and took 100 sleeping pills.

Often these cases bear a great deal of similarity to one another. The *Los Angeles Times* of April 18, 1953, reported "Skin Specialist in Morals Case Takes Own Life." Dr. Kenneth McLarand, age 47, was arrested by the L.A. police and pleaded guilty to the morals charges. He was set free on bail, returned home, and wrote a note to his wife saying, "I'm tired of it all." He then took an overdose of sleeping pills.

On April 19, 1954, the *Los Angeles Mirror* reported the case of another "suspected sex pervert" who stabbed a vice squad officer nine times when the officer attempted to arrest him. Albert Scheir, age 33, picked up the vice officer at a theater on Hollywood Boulevard frequented by gay men. The officer went with Scheir to his car; they drove to an empty, dark parking lot where the officer revealed his identity and demanded Scheir's identification. The gay man grabbed a knife and slashed the plainclothes officer, pushed him from the car and drove off. Scheir was later found lying on the front seat of his car, dead of carbon monoxide poisoning.[3]

The newspaper accounts are endless and describe the tragic deaths of gay men during a time, not radically different from our own, when public attitudes towards homosexuality presented gay people with few options in living their lives. Men who chose to have sexual affairs in public places or even chose only to meet partners in public places, risked police entrapment, observation and public exposure much greater than they face today. While the role of the police department and the legal system is obvious in coercing gay men into a no-win situation and truly driving some men to self-destruction, the media also must be held accountable for its role by publicizing these cases in a vicious and sensationalistic way. Terms such as "deviant activity," "sex pervert" and "child molestation" were used in even the most "liberal" newspapers, and the media did not hesitate to print occupations and home addresses of the men arrested. As recently as 1977, when gay men were arrested in Boston in what has been dubbed the "Boston Sex Scandal"—a politically motivated witchhunt targeting gay men as members of a "sex ring" which sexually exploited young men and boys—the *Boston Herald American* printed the names and addresses of the men who were arrested.[4] Many of these men later had all charges against them dropped, and the others were offered deals by an Assistant D.A. which allowed them to avoid trials and prison sentences.

Unfortunately, despite the attempts of the gay movement to put an end to the arrests and entrapment of gay men, such practices are not a thing of the past, and suicides brought on by such arrests still continue to plague the gay community. During August, 1972, a U.S. Naval officer was arrested in a men's room on the boardwalk in Atlantic City, New Jersey, and charged with sodomy. The man suffered much verbal abuse during his short stay in jail before he was bailed out by a friend. After mailing his brother his financial records and giving a friend his pornography collection, the man, aged 40, slashed his wrists and hung himself. Bill Bricker, president of Washington D.C.'s Gay Activists Alliance at the time, told the press, "This is one more case of an individual martyrdom on the altar of puritan prejudice. Some may say this man committed suicide. We know he was killed by the society which made him an outcast."[5]

During July, 1981, Boston police arrested 32 men and charged them with "open and gross lewdness" in an early-morning raid on a bar in that city's South End. Two weeks later, one of the men, described by friends as "very intelligent, very sensitive, very artistically oriented," took a large overdose of prescription medicine. Boston attorney John Ward, who was defending many of the men arrested, called the man's death "another gay murder."[6]

In May, 1980, William Oliver, a 38 year old civilian employee of the Army, was observed engaging in oral sex in a men's room stall by a Tyson's Corner department store security officer. The officer took Oliver to a county police officer who arrested him. Because Virginia's sodomy laws consider this activity a felony resulting in a permanent criminal record for the accused, in most situations the man is encouraged to plea bargain to a lesser charge, such as disorderly conduct. Fairfax County Attorney Robert Horan refused to allow a plea bargain from Oliver and scheduled a hearing on the sodomy charge. Oliver was found the following day in the kitchen of his apartment with a plastic bag over his head and a hose running from the inside of the bag to the gas stove.[7]

That men are forced to choose between what they preceive to be a life of ruin and disgrace as an exposed homosexual and ending their life through suicide, speaks to the absurdity of our culture's attitudes towards gay people. That so many men have chosen suicide reveals the overwhelming burden of stigma placed on openly gay people—a burden greater than many people can live with. Who is able to say that these men who chose suicide have made the wrong choice? The lives that awaited them may have included long prison terms, humiliating trials sensationalized by the media, disassociation from their families and professional disgrace. Men who have coped with such situations have often had to move from their homes and begin new, quiet lives, always fearing exposure again and being forced to build new identities. They are among the most obvious victims of a deeply homophobic culture.

The vulnerability of gay people to blackmail is also closely connected to suicide. While several branches of the government recognize this and use it as an excuse to refuse to give certain security clearances to lesbians and gay men, it is slowly becoming clear that, as long as a gay person is open about being gay, she or he is not vulnerable to blackmail. The prevalence of blackmail against gay people, however, has resulted in many women and men panicking and choosing suicide as a way out of a frightening and increasingly difficult situation.

On March 3, 1966, the *New York Times* reported on the operations of an extortion ring which had functioned throughout the nation for ten years and had blackmailed over 1,000 homosexual victims out of millions of dollars. At one point, two of the racketeers dressed as New York City detectives even walked into the Pentagon and walked out with a senior officer in the armed services in tow. This man, who had been blackmailed and had paid several thousand dollars to keep his homosexuality secret, eventually killed himself on the night before he was scheduled to publicly testify against his blackmailers before a New York grand jury.[8]

While blackmail of lesbians and gay men may seem like a crime of the past, it too continues to this day. One lesbian schoolteacher was driven to attempt suicide by a blackmailer who forced her to pay several thousand dollars in exchange for not revealing her lesbianism to the school's administration. The blackmailer, a former roommate of the woman, continued to threaten her with exposure, even after the suicide attempt. Recalling her attempt, the lesbian wrote:

> When I became conscious again after taking pills, I realized that there had to be another way out of the whole situation. It just wasn't worth killing myself over, but I felt so trapped. If I didn't pay her, she'd send a letter to the principal of the school and, in a small town in Georgia, gay people don't go over very well. I decided that rather than kill myself, I'd leave my job and leave town. I really loved teaching but I couldn't continue to do a good job with that hanging over my head. I packed up everything and moved to New York and started a new life. It wasn't a happy answer, but it was a lot better than killing myself.[9]

The fear of being exposed at one's workplace has played a major role in the suicides of many lesbians and gay men. Perhaps because gay people often invest a tremendous amount of energy in their work and create a cover to leave them safe from suspicions, exposure is deeply painful. Writing about the effects of such a double life for one woman, a lesbian writer stated:

> Some lesbians have so much invested in the cover they have built for themselves that when it is threatened, they can no longer live with themselves. Recalls the friend of one such woman, "One day they found her in the garage. She killed herself with carbon monoxide. A group of us tried to find out why. She didn't leave any note or sign. Eventually we heard that someone had threatened to expose her at work. I guess she just couldn't take it."[10]

The suicides of Charles Montgomery and his lover in San Francisco in the mid-sixties are examples of the way that exposure at work can push women and men who are already under tremendous pressure, over the brink. The story of Charles' life and death as a gay man is made more poignant because after his suicide his mother, Sarah Montgomery, became active in the gay movement and is well known as a founder of the Parents and Friends of Lesbians and Gays organization.[11]

From a very early age, Charles Montgomery appeared to be different from other boys. Music was an important part of his life from the age of three when he began playing tunes on the piano. By five he was composing songs and people were remarking on his great "sensitivity." His classmates in elementary school quickly labeled him "fairy" because of his gentleness, his love for music, and his disinterest in sports. He would often be scapegoated and challenged to fight by other boys on his way home from school. Because he needed to protect his hands for his piano playing and was raised to hate fighting, Charles refused to fight back. His mother was desperate to help her son and finally came up with the idea of encouraging Charles to rip the shirts of the boys who attacked him. "I knew that their mothers would punish them for the ripped shirts," Sarah recalled. It only took three ripped shirts and her son was let alone.

During his teenage years, Sarah realized that her son had been deeply harmed by the taunts and fighting. She was very disappointed that he refused to make music a career. Charles left home, moved to San Francisco, and married a year later. While he phoned his mother several times and confided to her his doubts that the marriage would ever work, he remained with his wife for several years and had four children. One time when Charles was playing with his infant son, Sarah recalled he said, "Thank God you won't have to go through what your dad has been through." While Sarah had been aware of feelings of conflict within her son, she could not imagine what caused him to feel such deep remorse. She detected his unhappiness and restlessness, but never understood its cause.

Charles worked as a carpenter, and he frequently refused to take on good professional jobs that would have placed him in a hierarchical work setting. He was offered an important position in the radiology department of a local hospital, but he turned it down. When he received an inheritance after his father died, Charles went into business with another man, buying, improving and reselling houses. The business did not go well; the other man left the state and Charles went bankrupt.

It was during this time, with family and financial demands becoming increasingly strong, that Charles first attempted suicide, leaving a note saying, "My family will be better off without me." He survived the attempt and went on to make another attempt by taking a large dose of phenobarbital, crawling into a culvert and passing out. He was discovered by a group of children and committed to a hospital. It was only after this second attempt that he called his mother and confessed the true nature of his unhappiness: he was gay, always had been, and could no longer lead a double life. He was 35 years old at this time.

Sarah reacted supportively, feeling guilty that her son had borne this trauma without her help. For Sarah, "The important piece of the puzzle finally fell into place."

Charles obtained a divorce shortly after his second attempt at suicide. His mother moved out to San Francisco where she found Charles living on Polk Street with his lover John. John was a traditionally masculine businessman who had a good, steady income. He had been with one company for 15 years and was one of their top administrators. John had not experienced the scapegoating that Charles had grown up with. Sarah moved in with the men; she "started to learn what it meant to be gay in a homophobic world." That was in 1962.

The men took Sarah to gay bars and to meetings of an early homophile organization, the Society for Individual Rights. She came to know the men and some of their friends very well and found that her son felt what she describes as "utterly horrible guilt towards his wife and his children for the double life he had led all those years." She grew to understand that his refusal to take high-powered jobs came from his fear of exposure by an employer or co-worker. While Charles now felt relieved to be able to be himself (he told Sarah, "Mom, you don't know how wonderful it is not to have to watch every motion of the hands"), he was still wracked with deep fear, guilt and shame. As John grew to trust Sarah and she heard his stories of fear and anguish, Sarah realized that these feelings were common for gay men in our society.

One night John came home from work and told Charles and Sarah that he had been demoted in his business to the original job which he had held 15 years earlier. He believed the demotion was due to his employer's finding out that he and Charles had recently purchased a small home together. John reasoned that the boss realized he was gay and demoted him, hoping he would quit the company. John was devastated by this. He and Charles had bought the house in order to live near Charles' children, who had become close to both men. When the demotion came, Charles felt extremely guilty. He came into Sarah's room that night and cried bitterly, telling his mother, "Oh, Mom . . . What have I done to this man?" Despite Sarah's attempts to comfort him, guilt poured out.

Sarah returned east shortly after this incident. Two weeks later, Charles, age 46, and John, age 48, went into their garage, sealed it, and turned on their car's motor. They were found dead two days later.

The suicides of these two men are clear examples of how the ramifications of "coming out," even in a subtle manner such as purchasing a house together, can bring on antigay discrimination and oppression that can push people over the brink. The men had somehow managed to cope with the stigma of being gay in America in the 50s and 60s—by moving to San Francisco (a "progressive" center for gay people, even at that time), choosing jobs carefully, and getting support from relatives and friends. Their lives had attained a precarious equilibrium that many gay people manage to live with throughout their lives. They were open enough about their homosexuality to live as a gay couple and socialize within gay circles, yet they maintained their cover during work and for unaware straight friends. This balance, because of the psychic and emotional energy required to make it work and the ability to accept a compromise of one's integrity, is very easily disturbed. The ramifications of John's exposure at work were too much for the men to bear—the balance was tipped and they lost their strength to cope with the discrimination directed at them. Society claimed two more victims in its campaign against homosexuals.

In order to prevent self-destructive behavior as a result of exposure of one's homosexuality, lesbians and gay men must continue to work to develop options that allow more people to feel comfortable "coming out." Much of this work is being done quietly throughout the country in small and informal organizations: support groups for lesbian mothers or married gay men, social caucuses in the workplace, networks of third world women or Jewish gay men, professional organizations for lesbian lawyers or gay physicians, etc. These groups allow gay people who share a common difficulty in coming out—dealing with their heterosexual spouses, for example—to discuss their experiences with one another in a safe and supportive environment. What is essential to the success of these groups is that women and men are allowed to make their own decisions about whether or not to "come out." An attitude of respect for an individual's personal ability to make this decision takes precedence over the political desirability of having more people become more open about their sexual orientation.

These groups are important for all lesbians and gay men, whether or not they themselves have participated in them. The fact that one is aware that there are other lesbian and gay teachers, for example, who meet and discuss such issues as surviving in a school system as a gay person means that all teachers have the option of getting such support if they need it. Faced with blackmail or exposure, one has options other than public disgrace or suicide; a person may get support that allows her or him to come out with dignity. The continued development of this option is essential to deterring panic in future situations.

Community response to mass arrests by vice officers may also be helpful in providing gay men with the support they need to survive the process of fighting unfair and homophobic charges. The tremendous work of gay men in the Boston area who organized the Boston-Boise Committee in response to mass arrests in their area provided the gay men who were victims of a corrupt district attorney and a sensationalistic press with enough support and legal assistance to get them through a long period of personal crisis.[12] While many members of the gay community hesitate to support men arrested for sexual activities in parks, bath houses, rest areas or with minors, it is apparent that mass community support may prove more effective and sustaining than the "hushing up" of such arrests.

Ultimately, lesbians and gay men will continue to be vulnerable to exposure until we have developed a thorough tolerance and appreciation of lesbianism and male homosexuality in our society. As long as there are laws which specifically target lesbians and gay men and as long as more generalized statutes such as statutory rape laws are primarily enforced against gay men, we will continue to see lesbians and gay men choosing suicide over facing a court trial. The fight for the removal of such laws is essential to deterring suicides due to public exposure.

Even more important, however, is the changing of the deeper attitudes that lesbians and gay men maintain about themselves. Until each of us appreciates our love for other women or other men as a valuable and positive part of our identities, we will be burdened with self-hatred and guilt. Affecting this change requires a great deal more than the alteration of laws and will take many, many years. The examples set by lesbians and gay men who have gone public with their sexual preferences can only help bring closer a time when we feel good about our sexuality.

Billie Jean King's disclosure of her affair with a woman, despite the flaws many lesbian and gay male activists have found in her public declarations, can only help millions of other people feel more able to discuss their homosexuality with friends and families. Five years before, a woman in King's position might have been forced to retreat in disgrace and shame. Instead, by maintaining her dignity and discussing her lesbian relationship with the media, King made an option possible for many people who have now, for the first time perhaps, seen a prominent person publicly accused of lesbianism admit the "crime" and survive.[13]

The importance of Billie Jean King's experience is impossible to deny. While she denied that she was a lesbian, King did admit to having a long-term lesbian relationship. As each individual lesbian or gay man faced with exposure deals with our enemies and detractors with increasing courage and honesty, the power and the potential for scandal is diminished. Options are developed and strengthened which may aid us all.

3.

Lesbian &
Gay Youth and Suicide

"We can't have people thinkin' Billy Joe MacCallister jumped off the Tal-lahatchee Bridge because of a man!*"—Bobbie Lee (played by Glynis O'Connor) in the movie* Ode to Billy Joe *(1976).*[1]

Several years ago a Los Angeles newspaper reported the sudden death of a young teenager. "Richard Roe" was a top student, a star runner on the track team, a winning debater—even a regular churchgoer at his family's fundamentalist Baptist church. He talked about going to a Baptist college after graduating from high school and was close to his family.

But something happened to Richard—an incident involving another schoolmate. He changed suddenly from a popular, outgoing personality to a brooding, defensive, argumentative one, shunning his family and friends. He stopped going to church, ran away from home three times—it seemed no one could communicate with him anymore.

One Tuesday afternoon—three years after the mysterious "incident"—Richard shot himself. His mother, who was in the family's kitchen, heard the shot and ran to his bedroom to find him already dead in a pool of blood. She explained to the press later that he had just wanted to be left alone for several years and she added that he had recently said, somewhat mysteriously, that there was no use trying anymore.

Nobody really knew what had happened three years before at school to change Richard's life. His mother wondered, "What did this boy do to my son? It's probably just as well that I don't know." His parents tried to get him to see a doctor, but he merely brooded about "that boy"; quitting the track team because "he" was on it, stopping his studies and learning martial arts to use, if necessary, on that same "boy." Without describing the transforming event, without drawing any conclusion, the newspaper story ends by noting that now Richard's tormentor was gone from him forever.

The facts of this article have been somewhat altered here, but the composite picture described is a familiar one. It is difficult for a gay person to read this and similar news reports and not wonder if the youth's suicide did not involve homosexual feelings or a sexual incident with the other young man.[2]

Recently, the suicides of children and youth have received increased attention from social service workers and the media. Statistics of suicides indicate that there has been a tremendous increase in the number of suicides of young people during recent years. National Institute of Mental Health statistics reveal that the suicides of young people between the ages of 14 and 19 increased 200% between 1960 and 1970.[3] During the same time period, suicides of men in their twenties doubled, and the rate for women in the same age bracket quadrupled. Suicide is now the third leading cause of death among young people, and many suicide experts believe it is actually the leading killer of young people. This is because automobile accidents are officially the leading cause of death among young people, though many of these "accidents" are undoubtedly deliberate suicides.

Despite the fact that some media attention has recently probed the suicides of young people, the relationship between homosexuality and youth suicide has virtually been ignored. Articles in the press on youth suicide are appallingly silent concerning issues of sexuality, and major studies of suicide among young people ignore or trivialize the subject.[4] One television producer who created a special show about adolescent suicide confessed, in confidence, that the production team had decided to eliminate all references to homosexuality from the show, despite the fact that several of the young people on whom the show focused were gay or were suffering deep conflict over their sexuality.[5] It is clear that taboos surrounding free and open discussion of lesbianism and male homosexuality are impeding people concerned about youth suicide from facing a major factor that is often involved. While suicide prevention workers have targeted specific youth populations as risk groups requiring special attention—runaways, drug and alcohol abusers, emotionally disturbed youth—too often they have avoided facing the fact that lesbian and gay youth are a population that greatly needs their attention and services.

Existing statistics indicate that lesbian and gay youth may experience tremendous feelings of self-destructiveness. In Bell and

Weinberg's study, over half of the lesbians and gay men who had attempted suicide had made the attempt at the age of 20 or below. A startling 36% of the black lesbians' attempted suicides had occurred when they were 17 years old or younger, as had 21% of the white lesbians', 32% of the black gay men's and 27% of the white gay men's.[6] In Saghir & Robins' study, five out of six homosexual men who had attempted suicide did so prior to the age of 20, or, as the authors state, "during the latter part of adolescent years, when conflict at home and with one's self concerning homosexuality was intense."[7]

It has been clear for some time that sexuality is a major factor in the suicides of young people. At the International Congress of Medical Sexology held in Paris in 1974, Dr. Klaus Thomas, in a paper entitled "Suicide and Sexual Disturbances," stated: "In juveniles, depressions and schizophrenia are far more rarely found than are neurotic illnesses which are generally combined with and/or caused by sexual troubles and anxieties. As a whole, undoubtedly the main reason for juvenile suicidal acts is sexual problems (in the broad sense of the word)."[8]

Dr. Robert S. Liebert, in a 1971 article in *Change* magazine wrote, "Virtually every male college student who has come to my attention because of a serious, and sometimes successful, suicidal attempt, has been either overtly homosexual or, at the time of the attempt, in a panic over his inability to repress his homosexual impulses, often towards roommates."[9]

Even columnist Ann Landers wrote, concerning young men who send her letters about their homosexual feelings, "Most of the boys who write are tortured with guilt and self-hatred. They live on the razor's edge, terrified that someone may learn they aren't like everybody else. Many who write are so ashamed of their physical desires for members of their own sex that they speak of suicide. One 17 year old Chicago boy wrote, 'If I can't get cured I would rather kill myself than be a pansy all my life.' "[10]

The unreliability of statistics on suicide and on the lesbian and gay male population has already been discussed. When those statistics are narrowed to lesbian and gay youth (people under the age of 21), they become even more distorted. Many of the young people who attempt or complete suicides have not even experienced overt sexual activity with people of their sex or have not identified themselves, publicly or privately, as lesbian or gay. Furthermore, the families of young people who kill themselves are often extremely concerned about how the public is informed of the situation, and, therefore, many suicides are publicly designated as "accidents," while issues of sexuality, and particularly homosexuality, are never mentioned.

A study performed in 1953 by Dr. A. Warren Stearns in Massachusetts looked at "cases of probable suicide in young persons without obvious motivation." These cases involved young men, "nearly all between the ages of eleven and sixteen, with a record of good health, good personality, good standing in the community, showing a good deal of leadership in their school life, who, for some reason not obvious, hung themselves. The pattern appears quite characteristic. They frequently take off their clothes, less frequently put on women's clothing; some tie themselves up . . ." Dr. Stearns cites specific cases of these bizarre suicides:

No. 6. Age, 15. Said to have been depressed for some time. Chained his hands and feet together with a heavy chain, put a chain around his neck and hooked it into a fall and tackle, climbed a ladder and stepped off, hanging himself. Following his death, at autopsy, his rectum was said to be dilated and a man was sent to prison for rectal intercourse with him.

No. 8. Age, 20. Of borderline intelligence. Found hanging in the woods, dressed in a man's jersey and shorts, white socks, army shoes, a woman's silk blouse and plaid skirt. Two women's slips were found nearby. Said to have frequently dressed up in women's clothes.

No. 25. Age, 14. A member of a group of boys who had a small clubhouse of old boards. Several of the boys said they did not like him very well as he was rough in the club, that he was usually quiet but got "mad" easily. However, at least ten boys who knew him were questioned by the police and they, and a boy who had slept in the clubhouse with him two or three times, noted nothing "queer" about him. His school reports were good . . . Found dead, hanging by the neck from a tree, an overturned 5 gallon pail under him. Dressed in female clothing . . . His own trousers, shoes and bicycle were nearby. Legs tied together at the ankles, below the knees and above the knees. Hands tucked in skirt belt behind body, all knots. Ankles tied in a length of gingham cloth. Silk stockings tied just below the knees and a few inches above the knees. At the mid-thigh a piece of gingham cloth held the thighs. A piece of cord tied about the upper right thigh. All knots in front. Numerous pieces of mirror glass below the body in a second girl's skirt. A third (knitted) skirt had been used to stuff the skirt to simulate female breasts. A cord used to encircle the breasts to accentuate them.[11]

Despite the repetition of the pattern that includes cross-dressing, Dr. Stearns offered no interpretation and instead stated, "It is to be hoped that further study will throw new light on these cases." No mention was made of sexuality, nor did the author probe issues of gender identification. The most that the good doctor seemed able to do was to present the gruesome cases and hope that others would draw some conclusions.

A similar failure to confront the factor of homosexuality in the suicide of a young person occurred recently in the case of James Dallas Egbert III, who received national attention in 1979 when he disappeared from Michigan State University and was widely rumored to be involved in a real-life version of the popular fantasy game Dungeons and Dragons. The national press pursued the story for weeks, although, even after his return home, the full story of Dallas' disappearance was never made public. About a year after his mysterious disappearance, Dallas put a pistol to his head and pulled the trigger.

The articles probing his suicide stressed that Dallas was a computer prodigy who entered college at 16 and was "so gifted that he had forged ahead of his teachers in computer courses." The *New York Times* article was given the headline "A Brilliant Student's Troubled Life and Early Death," and focused on the role the boy's brilliance played in his isolation from his peers. The article quotes high school teachers testifying to the young man's intelligence and his subsequent lack of social connections. A science teacher stated, "He was almost a caricature of a whiz kid, a little kid with big glasses carrying a big brief case and computers . . . Changing classes he was always walking by himself." While it is clear that intellectual personalities tend to become socially isolated among many adolescent peer groups, Dallas had another factor that contributed to his isolation— his classmates assumed that he was gay.[12]

The *Times* article includes all the information needed to understand the role homosexuality played in Dallas' feelings of alienation. A high school classmate said that, "People were pretty cruel to him," and described a school talent show that Dallas was in when some students in the audience began taunting him, "Tell them how queer you are!" At Michigan State University he joined the campus Lesbian and Gay Council and he was ostracized by other students. His roommate moved out. The newspaper's inclusion of this information indicates, to some extent, the recognition that these factors contributed to the motivation for his suicide, but the article fails to confront fully the issue of sexuality in several important ways. Al-

though it never states directly that Dallas was gay, it makes it clear
that he associated with gay people, was gay-baited by classmates, and
lived with a "homosexual" (but is certain to state that "the two had
not had a sexual relationship"). Perhaps this is due to the potential
liability of (and costs of defending) a law suit for libel, but it could
also be due to the failure of the author to recognize that a 16-year-
old person might actually be gay. Instead, the article implies that
Dallas' association with gay culture was a result of, rather than a
cause of, his confusion and social ostracism.

It is clear that parents, psychiatrists and writers concerned about
this young man's suicide are able to see the disparate pieces of evidence contributing to his suicide, yet are unable to acknowledge the
possible issue of Dallas' sexuality. This is unfortunately too often the
case with the suicides of young people who are struggling with
gender identification issues and issues of sexuality. The taboo surrounding homosexuality sometimes leads to a refusal to recognize
and verbalize the obvious. While some psychiatrists have explored
the connection between "homosexual panic" and youth suicide—or
people who are not gay-identified overreacting to a homosexual
incident or accusations of homosexuality—we have little clinical
information on young lesbians and gay men who have accepted their
homosexuality and suicide.

Printed below is a first-person account written by Stuart Kellogg, a
man in his thirties about his experiences with suicide attempts when
he was in college. The story is neither unique nor limited to the time
period in which it occurred. This account is presented because it
contains many elements that are common in the suicides and suicide
attempts of lesbian and gay youth and because the subject's reflections on his suicidal early years provide interesting information
regarding his motivation:

I first attempted suicide when I was 20 years old and a senior at
Yale. This was in October 1968, on the Monday following a weekend spent with my girlfriend and her parents at their summer
house. It is possible that my success with the parents and the
consequent plausibility of marriage to their daughter were final
straws, but my suicide had been inevitable for several months—a
low bird looking to perch.

On Sunday evening I took the train back to New Haven. During
that ride I began to dwell on suicide, carefully planning how to do
it. I also began to go the tiniest bit mad and to hope I would be
approached by "a homosexual." But I saw no likely man in the car.
(To be sure, had the train been full of gay people, I wouldn't have

recognized them. I knew no one who was homosexual, and I believed all the myths as to what homosexual men looked like, walked like, and did with their hands.) And besides, I wasn't actually looking for sex that night. What I craned my neck to see but did not see was an invitation to make a decision. So I reached New Haven alone and went to my college and to bed.

The next morning I went to the drugstore near the campus and priced sleeping pills. But I feared the checkout woman would stop me from buying the pills—a Yalie buying trouble at 9 A.M.—and so I went to the other drugstore, down by the New Haven green and well beyond the palisade of my known world. There I bought a bottle of Sominex.

Back at my college, I shut the door to my room—I shared a "double" with a friend; each had his own bedroom off the living room—took off all my clothes, and ate the pills. (This is not easy to do. The dust of that many pills sums up and becomes revolting, no matter what your mood. To this day I fear the powderiness of cheap aspirin.) Then I lay down on my bed and masturbated. For seven years I had proscribed, or at most rationed, my homosexual fantasies. But now I was dying and going where no one could criticize me, so for once I did exactly what I wanted. I thought of every swimming counselor, teacher, older boy, and peer I had ever loved or desired.

About noon I woke up, after having slept for about two and a half hours. I felt dreadful. I don't remember if I vomited. As it was clear I had not died or wasn't going to die neatly, I called the Department of University Health and told them what I had done. They said to come on over. Obediently I dressed and walked the five or six blocks to the DUH. While I waited by the nurse's desk, I grew scared that I would die after all. I knew I was losing my mind. At last the nurse spoke to me, and later a young doctor drove me to the hospital. The doctor had the sad gold eyes of a retriever; I felt I should cheer *him* up. He asked me to count backwards, to test if I had lost my faculties. Then we were driving into a circular driveway and at once I was on a hospital table where my stomach was pumped, while from the corners of the room four tall Gothic statues looked down and watched me. The doctors were laughing; but perhaps I only imagined their laughter, just as I had imagined the saints.

I spent the next three months in the Connecticut Mental Health Center. I was the best little patient in the world. In group therapy I talked of all my depressions except those attaching to homosexuality, and I was careful not to mention homosexuality itself. (As all passes and permissions were voted on by patients in a puppet democracy, we tried never to appear too distraught or to bring up issues disquieting to the group in general, lest we lose the right to go on walks or—worst of all—lest the administration of the hospital lock all the doors and restrict everybody to the ward, for our own good.) My doctor was terribly good-looking and the worst possible choice as a therapist for me. During our sessions he sat opposite me with his legs spread wide apart, a striking posture in anyone, let alone the therapist of a boy confiding his fears of homosexuality. As I soon learned that this doctor could not afford any talk of homosexuality, I dropped the subject and resorted to necessary, but easier, discussion of childhood depressions and angers. Two hospital aides, a man and a woman, were kind and would have listened to me, but I was fearful and would not give in to their attentions.

In early January 1969, as the hospital could only take patients for three months and as I appeared to be well, it was decided that I should look for a job in preparation for discharge. You must understand that I had never meant to be, I was not *designed* to be, anything other than a teacher, probably in a boarding school. Also, my homosexual desires were as strong as ever though still unrehearsed. So when I was faced with getting a job in a factory (my only likely employment, as a 21-year-old ex-patient with no B.A.) and with living the same repressed life I had once tried to quit, but now a greatly diminished version of that life, it seemed efficient for me to die. The hospital had proven their helplessness in the face of my sexuality and had also shown their scorn for homosexuality. I could look forward to no peace and no fun. To cease upon the midnight with no pain, was indicated.

So one morning when I was home from the hospital on a pass to job-hunt, instead of going to the factory where I had scheduled an interview, I took a bottle of aspirin from the medicine cabinet and, after making a feint at driving off, parked the car and walked into the fields. On a little rise where I had played as a child, facing the woods and away from all traces of humankind, I took the one hundred aspirin. I must have passed out, for I came to. I threw up and went back to my parents' house. There I threw up again. My father drove me to the local hospital and I was pumped out. The doctor on duty talked to me of Darwin and ecological niches. At the time this struck me as very odd or as hideously inappropriate.

As a result of this second attempt I entered the Yale Psychiatric Institute for extended treatment. There, too, homosexuality was considered *infra dig*; indeed, one foolish social worker forbad my stepmother to bring me flowers when she visited, lest flowers make me effeminate! Happily, my therapist was a civilized man and gently bullied me into doing something instead of just whining in the subjunctive. So I did kiss a man, and I didn't evaporate and my lips didn't fall off. Shortly after that I resumed classes at Yale and soon was discharged from the hospital altogether. All told, I was in mental hospitals for one year.

I made one more suicide attempt four years later. I was unhappy in a love relationship and felt trapped. This time, too, I took aspirin, in fact on the very same hill where I had tried earlier. In many ways this third attempt was a recalling of the past. (I was not hospitalized as a result of this stunt; probably wisely, as this broke the pattern.)

I have not been suicidal since: depressed, disappointed, but not suicidal in the old brooding way. I believe that a danger signal of impending suicide is when you commit adultery with death: when you sit at a crowded table or even talk with someone, but all your thoughts are given to conscious sleep. I have not done that for seven years.

I sometimes wonder if my suicide attempts could be called "homosexual" suicides. Would I have tried to kill myself had I not been homosexual? This is unanswerable, of course; but I do know that all three attempts were abetted by my unwillingness to confide in anyone out of fear that I would reveal my homosexuality in the course of tearful conversation. I can only imagine that had I felt freer to disclose my sexuality, then all the other ingredients of my depression would have had a chance to be aired and exorcized. But I trusted no one and so I talked to no one.

It is fun but barren to distribute blame—to blame society for stigmatizing homosexuality and to blame myself for not having had the wit, singlehandedly and without advice, to come out. More useful is to recognize that because the lack of role models almost proved fatal to me I should therefore come out now and encourage others to do the same. If I had known gay men and women, if my parents had included openly gay people among their friends, if my literature and history classes in school and college had acknowledged the homosexuality of so many of their heroes instead of denying it altogether or mentioning it coyly or as an example of leprosy overcome, I might not have tried to kill myself. Instead I did the sensible thing and tried to die, for who would want to live, if living meant a charade at best and exile at least?[13]

Stuart's attempts at suicide and his candid reflections on his self-concept during this period in his life raise several issues which pertain to the suicides and suicide attempts of lesbian and gay male youth. In particular, the isolation Stuart felt from others who shared his homosexual feelings and his total lack of awareness of homosexuals and homosexuality are a common experience in the lives of most lesbian and gay youth. The failure of American culture to go beyond the taboo associated with free and open discussion of homosexuality or to present same-sex relationships as a healthy and viable option leaves young gay people fully ignorant of a crucial aspect of their identity. What Stuart cites as a "lack of role models" is a dangerous factor contributing to depression and suicide among lesbian and gay youth.

While Stuart's teenage years occurred two decades ago, in the 1960s, before the development of the gay movement as we know it today, the situation for lesbian and gay teenagers today is not substantially different. Gay issues are still systematically excluded from the curricula of the overwhelming majority of high schools across the United States. Teachers who are lesbians or gay men and work, undoubtedly, in most, if not all, schools in the country, could be invaluable and accessible resources for young lesbians and gay men. They are prevented from serving this function in most places by their well-founded fear of dismissal if they reveal themselves to be lesbians or gay men. The situation is such that often when young gay people begin struggling with issues of sexual identity and go to a teacher they sense will be "sympathetic," the teacher may avoid the issue because of fear that aiding a student's "coming out" will result in public questioning of her or his own sexuality. This forces all parties into a no-win situation where the biggest loser is the student.

The failure of a school to support a gay teenager is obvious in the suicide of Kenneth Myers, a 16 year old entering 10th grade in Lebanon, Pennsylvania in 1977. In a suicide note, Myers explained that he was viciously taunted by his classmates and that his parents couldn't understand his anguished situation. His schoolteachers also provided him with no support. As summer vacation came to an end and the next year in a hostile high school loomed before him, Kenneth Myers put a gun to his head and killed himself. Local gay activists responded to the suicide and presented the school administration with copies of *Lesbian/Woman* and *The Gay Mystique*. Continuing to refuse to offer even token support or resources to lesbian and gay youth, the school's administration refused to put the books in the school library.[14]

The major difference between the 1960s, when Stuart was a teenager, and the late 1970s, when Kenneth Myers was a teenager, is the existence of a political movement of lesbians and gay men as well as cultures which are evolving from communities of women who love women and men who love men. Today there are women and men visible within the gay community who are able to serve as healthy models of the many different options lesbians and gay men are choosing in building their lives. However, because of the mainstream culture's failure to accept lesbianism and male homosexuality as viable life options, these women and men remain cloistered in their own communities and inaccessible to young people like Kenneth Myers. Lesbians and gay men who make important contributions to our society, beyond the gay movement, are rarely identified as gay by the media. Thus, the unaware young person still lacks access to adult models of gay lives. This can only serve to exacerbate the confusion and sense of isolation or difference that young lesbians and gay men face.

Another aspect of Stuart's experience with suicide that is common in the suicides and suicide attempts of gay youth is the failure of the medical profession to earn the confidence and trust of gay people. While some psychiatrists make big news of the American Psychiatric Association's removal of homosexuality from its list of sicknesses, before gay people of any age will have truly free access to health care, the medical profession has considerable work to do in the area of affirming lesbian and gay men and creating a medical agenda to meet their specific needs.

Thus the situation for suicidal lesbian and gay youth is often extremely difficult. Their feelings of sickness and worthlessness which lead them into suicidal states are confirmed by the very people who are claiming to offer treatment. While an occasional sympathetic social worker or psychiatrist may be found, the tales young gay people tell continue to confirm the traditionally antigay attitudes of health professionals. Lesbian and gay youth are vulnerable to this mistreatment to a greater extent than older lesbians and gay men because of the continued insistence on the part of "experts" in the field of adolescence that the concept of an adolescent who is gay is unthinkable. They insist on seeing adolescence as a time of flux, of "acting out" and "trying out," and they see homosexual feelings and activity during these years as "experimental" or "a phase." Young people who identify themselves as gay are often considered "rebellious" or are charged with "attempting to hurt their parents" and are rarely taken seriously. Thus the existence of a population of lesbian and gay adolescents is actually disputed by some health professionals—and access to medical services and facilities has never been awarded to nonexistent populations.

Though many young lesbians and gay men have attempted or completed suicides, many others have seriously considered suicide without acting on their feelings. The experiences of this group of lesbians and gay men are pertinent because of the thin line between the mental consideration of suicide and the actual suicide attempt.

The experience of a young lesbian who considered suicide at 19 tells much about the factors that motivate some young gay people towards suicide:

I came closest to suicide at 19, after my first woman lover broke up with me. I was in terrible pain over this, felt helpless, lost, anxious, unloved, abandoned, depressed, suffered sleep disturbance, felt like I'd lost part of myself, felt very lonely, and most importantly, as if my future was pointless and there was no reason for me to keep living. Obviously, my suicidal feelings were largely a result of having invested an extreme amount of emotional energy in my lover; I don't see this as a particularly gay-related phenomenon. However, there *were* several important ways that gayness fed into my problem:

a) My lover broke up with me for several gay-related reasons. She was having lots of trouble dealing with homophobia; I was starting to stick my nose out of the closet; she was threatened by this; also, she was uncomfortable with the extent of my emotional dependence on her, which (ironically) was largely a result of the fact that because of her fears of backlash, she did not allow me to talk very freely about me/us with other people who might have been able to support me. In other words, we were isolated together in her closet.

b) Since we were so isolated, I had no one to turn to to express my sadness, anger, hurt, no friends to spend time with after the relationship ended.

c) My parents didn't know about the relationship, so when I needed their support, I had to come out to them. My father gave me the homosexuality-is-sick line. My mother was less brutal but didn't really understand.

To summarize, then, the ways that I see my postrelationship suicidal ideation as gay-related:

1- The precipitating event (loss of relationship) occurred largely as a result of societal pressures against homosexuality.

2- My minimal resources for support in the time of crisis *were* so minimal largely because of the place of homosexuality in the society at the time in question (1976).

Although I did spend a lot of time fighting off death in 1976, I survived because my connections with people were, although minimal, not nonexistent. I worried a lot about the feelings of my survivors; I still cared about other people. I see this sense of connectedness as crucial in keeping depressed people alive.[15]

Mary's articulate thoughts on her experience with suicidal feelings reveal feelings of isolation, rejection and worthlessness which many suicidal people share. These feelings tend to cut across all sexes, races, sexualities, classes. Mary points out, however, that her isolation and low self-esteem were intensified because of her identification as a lesbian and the position in which this placed her in our culture. Mary had huge tasks before her: dealing with suicidal feelings and facing the rejection by her lover. If she was to get help from her family, hovever, she also had to take on another huge task—coming out to them. It is easy to see that this intensifies an already dangerous situation.

One of the major factors contributing to the suicides of lesbians and gay men is our estrangement from the traditional support systems within our culture that people turn to in times of crisis. For a young person, these institutions would ordinarily be their family, church and school. Because of the failure of these institutions to see homosexuality as a viable human option, these systems are usually not open to truly helping lesbian and gay male youths. In fact, they have lead the way in stigmatizing young lesbians and gay men. The family has reacted to gay youth often by kicking the teenager out of the house. The church has asked her or him to repent, and schools have attempted to deny gay youth access to facilities and school events. If young gay people are deprived of these traditional support systems, where can they receive the help and support they need?

Mary had connections who were able to provide the support she needed, but she was in a fortunate and rare situation. In the absence of the traditional systems, young lesbians are often left to flounder on their own or, when they become particularly desperate, seek help from an institution that they know will not help them and which will, in fact, often intensify their feelings of conflict and self-hatred. New options need to be created.

Such options have started to be developed over the past ten years and may provide a valuable resource for lesbians and gay men under the age of 21. Lesbian and gay youth programs which provide young people with a social experience that is affirming have sprung up in urban centers around the country. These groups, which range from well-funded social service programs to informal networks of rap groups meeting in bars or in church basements, seem to be the key to the future of developing young gay people who are able to cope with the oppression they face. Most of these groups are offering peer counseling and group counseling experiences where young people can find others whose lives are similar to their own and get the support to meet the challenges directed at them by a hostile society. Many of these programs provide referrals to counselors and psychiatrists for those young people who need more intense counseling or are in need of specific treatment.

Unfortunately, access to these groups, at this point, is limited in many ways. Often they are publicized only through the gay and feminist press, so a young person has to have access to these periodicals to know about them. Since these groups are mainly in urban centers, rural youth or young people without access to transportation are often unable to connect with them. Until the programs are publicized in schools, youth programs, churches and clinics, their ability to reach the population they are targeted to serve will be limited.

On a deeper level, a young person will generally need to be self-aware enough as a lesbian or gay man before being able to consider joining these groups. This is, itself, a major step for a person and one which tends to be made primarily by those who feel good enough about themselves to take the step. The existence of lesbian and gay youth groups can only help to move young people closer to identifying themselves in a positive way as lesbians and gay men. The success of these groups throughout the country will play a major role in aiding depressed and suicidal gay youth in the future.

4.

Suicide and Activists

"So after six months out of the closet, as a reasonable success in the gay world . . . I discovered I was as lonely and isolated as ever. Then I started to freak."
—*Michael Silverstein*

Perhaps no myth is so dangerous to lesbians and gay men as the myth that claims that the act of "coming out" as a gay person provides a person with a margin of insurance against self-hatred or self-destructiveness. This myth leads many lesbians and gay men to believe that, once able to be open about their homosexuality, their personal problems and anxieties will all fall by the wayside. Coming out is looked on as a miracle cure, a salvation from all shortcomings and malaise.

There *is* a germ of truth to this myth. Many resources that are essential elements of improving one's self-image as a lesbian or gay man become available once one's gay identity is acknowledged. Without such acknowledgment, a person is often unable to receive the support services that are specifically tailored to her or his needs. Exposure to other lesbians and gay men who are happy with their sexual orientation is another benefit of accepting one's sexuality and integrating oneself into the lesbian and gay community.

However, merely becoming open about one's love for others of the same sex will not insure a person against destructive tendencies. While suicides of lesbian and gay male activists are not common, several suicides within the activist community have occurred, and they reveal the complexity of issues related to politically active lesbians and gay men.

Claudia Scott, a poet and activist in the Chicago and Philadelphia lesbian communities, and Michael Silverstein, a gay activist in New York City and San Francisco, were very different people. While Claudia grew up in rural farm communities in Oregon, Michael was raised in Oakland, California. Michael pursued a career in academia, while Claudia became a poet and a carpenter. Michael viewed himself as an enlightened gay man on issues of sexism, but his political vision was quite different from Claudia Scott's lesbian-feminist viewpoint.

There are, however, similarities that are striking and make these two people valuable figures in any study of lesbian and gay male suicide. Both Michael and Claudia had attained reputations in the lesbian and gay male community—locally and nationally—and their suicides both received coverage in the lesbian and gay press.[1] Both people were prolific writers and left substantial written material—published and private—that discussed feelings of depression and suicide. Thus we have sufficient documentation to compile the facts and provide some analysis of their suicides.

The fact, however, that Claudia Scott was a woman and Michael Silverstein was a man must be kept in mind in any analysis of their suicides. While both suicides involved people active in the lesbian and gay movements, studies have shown that the suicides of women and men are quite different in many important ways—including the rates of suicide and suicide attempts and the method of committing suicide.[2] While many forms of violence are common within the male population, suicide is one of the rare forms of violence that is viewed in some ways as a "culturally acceptable" option for women,[3] yet in other ways it defies societal expectations of women. As Phyllis Chesler writes:

> Physical action—even the exquisitely private and *self*-destructive act of taking one's own life—is very difficult for women. Conditioned female behavior is more comfortable with, is defined by, psychic and emotional self-destruction . . . Suicide *attempts* are the grand rites of "femininity"—i.e. ideally, women are supposed to "lose" themselves in order to "win." Women who succeed at suicide are, tragically, outwitting or rejecting their "feminine" role, and at the only price possible: their death.[4]

Thus though it may be easy to see similarities in the suicides of Claudia Scott and Michael Silverstein, it is important to keep the distinctions in mind.

Claudia Scott was born on October 31, 1948, into a Fundamentalist Christian family.[5] She was the eldest of seven children and the family lived in Southern California until Claudia was ten. They then moved into an Oregon farmhouse that the family had inherited. It appears that most of the children in the family were influenced by their parents' religious and political views, and several of Claudia's brothers attended Bible colleges in the South.

Claudia's journals from her high school years reveal both that she was a godfearing young woman and that, unlike many young people from similar Christian backgrounds, she had a strong, independent streak. While she was academically quite successful in school and became co-valedictorian of her high school class, Claudia was haunted by a sense of separateness and alienation from others. During her senior high school year, she wrote in her journal:

> Things have seemed so disjointed lately—they don't tie together—there's no unity, no purpose. I have the feeling I'm just existing, just passively letting everything just roll over me and I'm not participating at all.—February 22, 1966[6]

Although it is impossible to assess the basis for the feelings of alienation that plagued Claudia at various times during her life, one factor that may have contributed to her early feelings may have been a growing awareness of her intense feelings for other young women. The high school journals focus primarily on Claudia's relationship with her best girlfriend and reveal a love that is both naive and explicit. Her interest in Lily during those years was clearly an obsession for her and the journals show that Claudia's moods were often dependent on her friend: Lily's successes sent Claudia into heaven; a day without seeing her friend left her wounded and sad.

There is no evidence in the journals that Claudia was able to see this relationship as including an erotic component. Once Claudia was away from her family and her conservative Oregon community and transported to college at Washington University in St. Louis, however, she was able to develop an attachment with a friend that included sexual involvement. Perhaps what is most striking about the college journals is Claudia's ability to confront her lesbianism and cope with the societal ramifications that face women who love women. During her first year in college, when she was eighteen, Claudia wrote:

> Last night I went out to Maryhurst to talk to Jill, supposedly because she was worried about me, but I found out she was more worried about herself, her relationship with Karen. Theirs is homosexual too—it was really a surprise for both of us—but the difference is that they feel guilty about it. It's bad enough to be pitted against society when you believe you are right and have confidence in yourself, but when you know you're wrong, then something has to give. And so Jill and Karen have got to quit or else quit their religion. We have to quit or quit society, but that's a much easier choice to make, at least for me. I'm resigned and [unrecognizable word] for my life.—April 9, 1967

Friends of Claudia's later in life reported that Claudia had expressed to them feelings that her acceptance of her lebianism in college was comparatively easy. Nothing in the journals of this time indicates that her lesbian feelings made her feel the self-hatred and doubt that many young lesbians face. Her college relationship brought her joy and sadness, yet her feelings seemed more related to her lover's ambivalence about the relationship than to her own lesbianism. Claudia's lover also dated men during the three years they were together and, while the relationship seemed to progress positively through their college years, shortly after the time of their graduation, Claudia's lover married. This appears to have been a great disappointment to Claudia and, having received her degree in linguistics and literature, Claudia moved to Chicago, a city she saw as more sophisticated than St. Louis and one with a women's community she could become involved with. Thus Claudia sought to recuperate from the demise of the relationship by moving and by entering new activities.

Claudia's five years in Chicago were an important time for her. She began seriously to write poetry and began publishing her work. A collection of poems, *Portrait*, was brought out by a local press during the summer of 1974.[7] She conducted workshops at an annual lesbian writers conference and worked as a layout and production volunteer on *Lavender Women*, a local lesbian journal. In a biographical statement published by Claudia in the October, 1974, issue of *Lesbian Tide*; she wrote:

> Everyone has parents, was born somewhere, raised by someone and managed somehow to survive. And it's all really important only in terms of what one makes of it *afterwards*. I got a lot of strength and self-confidence from my family, and these days, I ignore their expectations along with most everyone else's . . .
>
> I'm basically a poet in love with words. I spend my time crafting them into images, into portraits of the moments of interaction between people, the fractional revelations of who they are. Mostly the people are women because generally I like women better than men. Which must be the reason I'm a lesbian . . . My first book is called *Portrait*. It was just published this summer and it's all very exciting. Basically, I take my vitamins every day, try to avoid telling anyone else what to do, and hope to live a long and happy life.[8]

During her stay in Chicago, Claudia became involved in her second intense love affair and the relationship again brought on confusing and ambivalent feelings. Her journal entries during these years reveal feelings that the relationship demanded too much from her and that she felt she and her partner were too different to remain together. During a visit the women made to Claudia's family home, Claudia's parents attempted to draw her back into the family fold and Claudia reacted by withdrawing into herself.

During the summer of 1976, when the relationship had changed from love affair into friendship, Claudia met a woman named Frances Hanckel at the American Library Association convention, where they were both involved in the ALA's Gay Task Force program. Claudia soon moved to Philadelphia to be near Frances and brought to the relationship the same powerful and obsessive needs that had been a part of her previous relationships.

Shortly after the move to Philadelphia, Claudia sank into a depression that she recorded in her journal:

> But now to face another issue. I am very depressed. Not just today, this is over the long haul. This depression has been recurring for two months . . . I'm very happy when I'm with her. But what does this happiness mean? What relation does it have to my larger life? Where is my larger life if it comes down to that? And I think it does. I haven't caught my stride here yet. I moved here because of Frances. But I have to have something else to do and I haven't just found it.—January 2, 1977

Claudia's awareness that she was overly dependent upon her primary relationships for her happiness was growing. Coupled with this awareness was the realization that, beyond such a relationship, she felt empty. In an attempt to remedy this feeling, Claudia became more involved in Philadelphia's lesbian and gay community. She became a founding member of the city's Sisterspace Lesbian Hotline and took responsibility for training new phone volunteers. Around this time, Claudia came into a family inheritance and purchased a house in West Philadelphia which she proceeded to rebuild. As she went about building a new garage roof, adding a wood stove to her house and installing stained glass windows, it became clear to friends that the house had attained a symbolic significance in her life. As Frances recalled, "It seemed that she invested so much in the house, with the hope that somehow it was going to anchor her."[9] Claudia developed her carpentry skills through her work on the house and began to teach courses on woodworking and home repair for the Free Women's School. She later helped to renovate the new home of Giovanni's Room, Philadelphia's lesbian and gay bookstore which serves also as a community center.

Claudia continued to develop her strong interest in writing poetry, and her poems, which generally appear to be deliberately removed from her personal life experiences, occasionally reveal the conflict and depression that festered inside the poet.[10] These were, however, feelings that she did not share with friends, and, in fact, most women close to her were shocked to learn of the deep feelings of pain and conflict that Claudia held inside. Laurie Barron, who Claudia lived with when she first moved to Philadelphia, expressed the feelings of many of Claudia's friends when she said, "The Claudia we all knew was very different than the Claudia from the journals. They seemed like two different people."[11]

Wendy Galson, another friend, said that Scott "always seemed to be cheerful, strong and settled." Still another friend insisted that "Claudia was always the rock."

Claudia's poetry was published in several feminist journals, including *Conditions* and *Sinister Wisdom*, but she was frustrated by her inability to place a new manuscript of poems with a publisher.[12] She was affected by her frequent rejections by publishers and editors, but joked about these rejections to friends. She made a collage out of the rejection slips and also wrote a poem excerpting the contents of these notes.[13] She joined a lesbian writers group but remained just as closed about her deeper feelings to these women as she did with her other friends.

Claudia's relationship with Frances developed and had its good periods and its bad periods. It became clear after three years, however, that Claudia was not going to be able to have her tremendous needs met by her partner. Looking back on the relationship, Frances summarized the problems: "We were each afraid of losing control, of passing that last intimate emotional barrier. We almost worked it through, but I pulled back. We never found a way to resolve this deep barrier, but continued to have a close, loving friendship."

Claudia seems to have been deeply affected by the failure of this romantic relationship during the winter and spring of 1979. Her long-term feelings of emptiness and lack of direction came to the surface. In one journal she planned out the week ahead, wondering how she would be able to distract herself from her feelings of depression:

> What am I going to do?
>   Monday—nothing
>   Tuesday—nothing, until evening, then writers' group
>   Wednesday and Thursday—nothing
>   Friday, Saturday, Sunday, Monday morning—Washington.

Claudia and Frances seemed to struggle together as they nego-
tiated their change from lovers to friends. Claudia sank into depressions which brought up her feelings of disappointment in all her
romantic relationships. In a letter to Frances, Claudia wrote: "You
think/feel that I don't trust you. It is an old, old habit. It has gotten
me through a lot. If you ask for very little, accept what's offered,
expect nothing, you are seldom disappointed."

At various times through this time period, Claudia became overtly
depressed. Because she was acutely aware of these depressions, yet
felt helpless to do anything to improve her condition, she began to
panic. Her depressions became desperate and called up all her
feelings of alienation:

> There are people who care about me.
>   I could call them up & spend time with them
>   but what would it mean.
>   I would come home again and then what
>   How many of them would I tell that I am seriously
>   depressed, that I don't know what to do with my life.
>
>   I went skiing with Carolyn & Margaret and
>   when we were skiing it was fine, the rest
>   of the time it was all I could do not to
>   fall apart.
>
> That's my life all right, it's been like that for years.
>   How was it different during our relationship, that
>   I liked it better and I don't like it now.

This entry reveals Claudia's awareness of her inability to confide in
others about her depression. She was also unable to explain to her
friends about the changing nature of her relationship with Frances.
When Frances slowly began to set limits on the relationship, Claudia
reacted with strong feelings of anger and panic, revealed primarily
in her journals. She also continued to be intensely aware of her
"strategy" to salvage the love affair. During the spring, the journal
entries appear as the strategic map of her thoughts on Frances: "F.
returning from DC . . . will she call? What will I tell her of my
weekend?"

Claudia goes on to weigh the positive and negative sides of various
reactions she could have to the situation. Pages of the journals are
filled with her analyses of phone conversations she had with Frances
and it becomes clear that Claudia had become obsessively focused on
the termination of the relationship. As it became more clear to
Claudia that the relationship must change (Frances told her, "But I

cannot, won't go too far. Our problem seems to be that what is too far for me, isn't enough for you."), Claudia's panic increased. While she had never been in therapy before, Frances suggested that she seek help and finally Claudia consented. The counseling did not last many weeks, but when Claudia finished, Frances recalled, she seemed "in much better shape." While many of her friends sensed that Claudia was on the road to recovery during the summer, her writings reveal otherwise. They show her continued obsession with the break-up of the relationship. In one poem, she considers moving from Philadelphia, as she had moved from St. Louis and Chicago before:

> I could move on
> it's what I've done before
> I know my way around
> three cities now
> and there are still more
> I could tie up this one
> friends, clubs, job, house
> these three years of my life
> and move
> I've done it everytime before
>
> pulling myself away
> things haven't worked out
> with another person
> I tried, I'll try again elsewhere
> I'm ok, still strong and
> self-confident enough to move
> forgodsake, I'll be just fine[14]

But Claudia was not fine, nor was she able to continue to run from city to city to avoid the aftermath of her love relationships. As much as she preferred to calm herself by reaffirming her strength and self-sufficiency—which she wanted in order to protect herself from the pain of her very real needs—and turning to her friends for help and support, there seems to have been a continuous struggle raging in her mind:

> so what I really want to talk about is support networks, the being able, becoming able, having become able to reach out to other people in a disaster; withdraw, turning in to myself only, being ultimately self sufficient & proving it by moving away
>> (hm, is it not a form of suicide—or at least is that not the aspect I want to stress—but rather a proof, to myself, that I'm

fine, strong enough to move forgodsake, still self sufficient, not ruined by this disaster—it & everything connected w/it can be wrapped up in a little package, an experience, a few years in my life & my life seen as a succession of these)

As Claudia continued to dwell on the failure of her relationship, she experienced what seems to have been deep, uncontrollable pain. The final four months of her life appear in the pages of the journal as a tortured time when Claudia seemed extremely self-aware, yet helpless to ease her pain. She made feckless attempts to reach out to her friends from the Sisterspace Lesbian Hotline and the writers' group. Claudia called Laurie Barron to arrange a dinner with Laurie and her lover Marcy Muldawer, indicating that she had something to discuss with them, but during the evening, Laurie recalled, "We talked and laughed and had a nice time. But absolutely *nothing* came out." Marcy met Claudia for a series of lunches in November and December and remembers that "Claudia was seriously upset, obviously different, but she said nothing about it and I didn't ask." Ironically, Frances assumed Claudia was talking with the writers' group about her depression.

In November, Claudia traveled to Texas to spend Thanksgiving at her brother's house and to see her newborn niece. Claudia's parents drove down from Oregon and the visit turned into a disaster for her. Her parents attempted to reclaim her for the family and they all fought terribly. The visit left her with feelings of permanent estrangement from her family and with additional feelings of loss and anger.

As the Christmas holiday approached, Frances recalls that Claudia seemed "in much better spirits than during the summer." The two had spent the past three Christmas holidays together and Frances was aware that the holidays could be tough for Claudia. She attempted to make plans with Claudia to join her at several events during Christmas week, in an attempt to show that, while the relationship had changed, they were still special friends.

Claudia did not see things this way and, in fact, was feeling increasingly shut out from Frances' life. In early December, Claudia began looking towards the holidays apprehensively:

> She asked if I was going to spend Christmas with them, whoever them might be. I said we hadn't discussed it, she said she'd just assumed. I guess I will. In my current state I'm dreading it...
> —December 9, 1979

Frances needed to alter her holiday week plans with Claudia a few days later. While Frances recalled that Claudia seemed open and understanding of these changes, the journal reveals that Claudia was angered and worried:

> She had bad news—she has a hospital Christmas party the Saturday night we were supposed to spend together. She asked if I wanted to go, but I don't. So she said she would come over Sunday afternoon. We'd do a puzzle in front of the fire, have dinner, go over to her house, give each other presents and then hang the prints. Yes, that should be a very nice day. If it could just be on a Saturday instead of a Sunday, it would probably be perfect . . .
>
> We had talked at dinner about Christmas, what I should get her parents, but Joy had not been mentioned. I took her to the subway this morning and asked at some point if she was going to be there. She had finally decided over the weekend, that she would. I served notice last night that I wanted to see her Christmas tree. I also want to see her again, and her apartment, all of that, be on a bit more solid footing before Christmas. I think it will be a good Christmas if we make it so, but if we just assume it will happen, there's entirely too much potential for disaster.—December 12, 1979

From this passage, it appears that Claudia was aware of the potential for danger during the holidays. Unfortunately, she was unable to instigate plans with anyone besides Frances that would allow her to have a happier holiday. She methodically plotted out when she would see Frances for the holidays—where it would be, what they'd do, who would join them. At the same time, she was feeling more distant than ever from Frances. Five days before her suicide, Claudia wrote in the journal:

> She has cancelled or postponed or abbreviated everything we've scheduled together this month, except for the Messiah, which she wouldn't miss if she were dying. I feel very expendable in her life.—December 18, 1979

Around this time, Claudia also seems to have begun to be confused about time. Her journal entries for December 16 and 17 are listed as "11/16" and "11/17" rather than"12/16" and "12/17." Previous December dates are listed with the "12" and this may reveal Claudia's developing confusion or perhaps her unconscious wish to put off the imminently approaching holidays. While it is impossible to interpret this dating error with any certainty, it is important to acknowledge what appears to be the only dating error this author could find in Claudia's journals.

As the weekend before Christmas approached, Claudia's journal entries stopped. Her weekend schedule included plans to see Frances and Frances' new partner Joy on Friday evening and on Sunday afternoon. Friday evening's dinner seemed to go generally well. Frances recalled, "We had a lot of fun. It was a really good time." And Claudia seemed to like Joy and enjoy her time with the women.

We have no account of Claudia's actions after she returned home from the dinner. A neighbor saw her go into her garage around 1:00 a.m. and she appears to have connected a hose to her car's exhaust pipe, sat in the car, and asphyxiated herself.[15]

Frances arrived for her visit with Claudia on Sunday afternoon. She did not find her in the house and went out to the garage where she discovered the body. The medical examiner would later list Claudia's death as "carbon monoxide poisoning."

Michael Silverstein's suicide in 1977 sent shock waves through the gay community. Silverstein was seen as a leader and activist and was a writer on movement issues. His death brought strong reaction in the gay press. Activist Bill Beasley is quoted in San Francisco's *Crusader* as saying, "The death of Michael Silverstein was a tragedy, he gave so much of himself, and this only leaves me to wonder, did we in the gay community give enough of ourselves to Michael when he really needed us? Did someone fail to say hello when Michael needed a friendly word? A senseless act. We all shall miss him!"[16]

While the gay press exhibited the same disbelief and outrage that traveled coast-to-coast among many gay activists, those people who knew Michael personally, and knew his writings, were well aware that he had been grappling with feelings of depression and suicide for a long time. The suicide is made both more tragic and more fascinating because of the extensive personal writings Michael left that concerned his feelings about being a gay man and the formation of his political and his personal identity. Throughout these essays it is clear that he was frequently confronting issues he saw in terms of life and death and was engaged in a constant struggle to stay alive.

Michael grew up in Oakland, California, and seems to have experienced gender-role conflict from an early age.[17] "By the time I was ten," he wrote, "the central fact of my life was the demand that I become a man."[18] Michael felt his difference from other boys deeply and was painfully aware of his inability to fulfill the traditional masculine role which boys are indoctrinated into. He developed an identity as a "sissy," an identity he accepted with much pain and regret:

One could only succeed at establishing his manliness or be a failure, a sissy, someone who couldn't stand up and fight. One didn't choose to be a sissy, a loser—one lost. Since manliness was, of course, what everyone would want, the unmanly must be those who were too weak to make it as a man.

By the time I was in junior high, I defined myself and was defined by the other boys as a loser, as the class sissy. Largely this meant that I saw myself as a failed man. Yet (I now realize) the beginning of my Gayness was the beginning of my attempt to choose to be what I was. I began to redefine myself positively, to redefine what it meant *not* to be a successful man. In so doing, I was moving outside the social reality I had been born to.[19]

In direct reaction to his gender-role identity conflict, Michael moved towards an identity that was both functional for him and socially acceptable—the role of "the Brain." While this role allowed him to function successfully in a capacity appropriate to the socialized role of men, it kept him alienated from much of his true identity and in what a friend of his termed "incredible, lethal spiritual isolation."[20]

His writings are filled with remembrances of the pain he experienced as a boy who was not traditionally masculine. He repeatedly recounts the painful feelings he faced from every corner because of his failure to act as boys "should": to compete and fight, to "own women" and "own the world": "My parents, my friends, my teachers told me that I was a victim, a loser, I must lose in a world where only the winner is a Man, a human being. I was not a real Man. I was a queer, a half-Man, a pseudo-Man, like a woman. I could never aspire to the dignity accorded only to the conqueror, the Man on top."[21]

An identity battle raged within him through high school, college and through graduate school at UCLA. Michael's ability to succeed academically won him some of the praise and some of the validation he lacked as a boy. As he won prestigious fellowships and bandied about his verbal skills, Michael found that he was finally "winning" and enjoying it. As he later recalled, "For the first time in my life I had some taste of power over others."[22]

After graduate school, Michael won an appointment in CCNY's Sociology Department and he moved to New York in September, 1967. It was at this time that his identity as a "Brain" began to cause increasing conflicts for him. The intense social and emotional isolation he had been immersed in for years began to plague him constantly. His needs overwhelmed him and he did not find the degree of friendship and support he needed from his academic colleagues.

He looked to his students to fill these needs and he cultivated an identity that would draw the students to him. He became politically radical and identified strongly with youth culture. On campus he was seen as a "guru," "father-figure" and "host." He was immensely popular with radical students and he found support and love—some of which he felt was false and some which was real:

> Sometimes I did manage to establish real human contact. There are people—students and colleagues—whom I love, and who love me, whom I met while I was teaching. I'm still in contact with some of them. We've talked about the past, and have gone on to more authentic relationships. To dismiss the four years of experience I've just come from is not only unfair to myself, but to many other good people. In spite of everything, there was some real human contact, some authentic friendship, some little love.[23]

It was during this time that Michael's struggle with his homosexuality came to the forefront. He felt an overwhelming need for attention and affection from men and could not be satisfied with the "safe" relationships he had with heterosexual men. The situation became incredibly difficult as he became close to his students and felt even greater needs toward men. He later explained his dilemma: "Even with all my desperation, I still couldn't see any space for change, any place to go."[24]

Michael explored his inability to identify himself with society's image of homosexual men in several of his essays. He captured concisely the difficulty homosexual men have faced in identity-formation because their entire knowledge of homosexuality has been formed from insults, derisive jokes and pity. Michael wrote, "The message that came across was that they [homosexual men] were pitiful, crippled, tormented creatures, always good for a laugh ... Since it was tremendously important for me that I take myself seriously, I was completely unwilling to see myself as part of a group depicted as vain, frivolous, childlike, foolish—or as a tormented, mutilated metaphor for human loneliness."[25]

A friend, writing after Michael's death, described his life to this point:

> Being gay, being a sissy, being a brain, being a good boy, being an academic who lived at home and wrote his sociology dissertation on alienation among intellectuals (he interviewed, among others, Anne Sexton); having Good Taste (woven hangings, Chinese prints), wanting to be impressive and never showing a feeling and never taking a stand ... And all the time running to

shrinks begging to be cured of being gay, so he could have a family like everybody else.

"God it was lonely," he wrote.[26]

The tension between Michael's need for emotional intensity from men and his desire to maintain a public image of respectability broke in 1969. At the November Peace March in Washington, he experienced his first confrontation with gay liberation. A group of five men were marching with a gay liberation sign and, Michael later recalled, "They didn't look ridiculous, silly or grotesque. They were talking to one another like friends; they didn't seem tormented, lonely, miserable. They were people, like me, at a peace march, and proud of being Gay. They looked like people I could talk to about serious things, about my life."[27] Michael saw a place for himself.

He went to a meeting of the Gay Liberation Front in New York City and began to find other gay men he could, to some extent, identify with. He became very involved in the political discussions and debates at these meetings and his gay consciousness developed quickly. Michael's description of the changes his feelings underwent is a telling portrait of the discovery of gay rage:

> All the self-hate of our isolation started to turn outward in a growing torrent of rage. I had never really hated anything before—except part of myself. Now I began to hate this society, and I began wanting to destroy all of it. It was this wave of rage that finally broke through the conditioning of a lifetime, and what had seemed true and unalterable before now appeared as something monstrously evil that must be destroyed. I hated what this society had done to me, then what it had done to us.[28]

It was during this time that Michael's own sexual attractiveness surfaced as an issue for him. One former GLF member described Michael as being "fat and dumpy" and unattractive. Michael wrote, in an essay entitled "The Politics of My Sex Life," about his self-consciousness during these days:

> I had been in the bars a few times, enough to know I was a loser there. I wasn't pretty enough to get the sexy guys to sleep with me. But gay liberation was made up of people like me; they sat around and argued and discussed things. This was the game I could win at. So I came out, talking . . . A surprisingly large number of pretty boys were willing to go to bed with me . . .[29]

Allen Young, who was a member of GLF during these days, recalled that Michael was very self-conscious of his physical appearance. Young said, "Michael was a Jewish, left-wing intellectual and he looked the part. Looking as Jewish as Michael did can be difficult in the gay community. American beauty standards are anti-Semitic and, in the gay community, the beauty standards are anti-Semitic."[30]

As Michael became immersed in the rising tide of gay liberation, he gave more and more of his energies to the movement and less and less to his academic career. He came up for tenure at CCNY and it was not granted. Some people believe that this happened because of "unprofessional behavior"; others because of his radical politics; others because of his homosexuality. He was one of eight sociology department faculty members terminated that year and student radicals seized a building on campus to protest the dismissal.

This was a very difficult time for Michael. In addition to losing his job, he was running up against some difficult and painful realizations. After joining and becoming an active part of the gay liberation movement, Michael was realizing that "liberation" was not the answer to all of his problems. And gay men, from whom he had been isolated so many years, were not the saviors he imagined them to be. In fact, they too were unwilling or unable to satisfy his prodigious needs: "So after six months out of the closet, as a reasonable success in the gay world, that is, having a fair amount of sex with relatively desirable guys, I discovered I was as lonely and isolated as ever. Then I started to freak."[31]

He became extremely vulnerable, paranoid, and his needs persisted as strongly as ever. A new job at California State College at Hayward lasted only a year, again dismissed amid rumors—that he "had failed to develop a professional self-image"[32] and identified with the students; that his "radical approach to teaching" or his gay liberation politics were unacceptable at the school. His entry into the Berkeley political scene had been impressive but he continued to feel unsatisfied:

> For a year I put all my life into gay liberation, and at the end of the year I felt as bad as I had before. I had no lovers, no friends I really trusted, and was being stripped of all the symbols of success I had had before as their meaninglessness became increasingly obvious. I couldn't be a teacher any more because I could no longer pretend to be strong and self-sufficient. It was too late to put the mask back on. I couldn't pretend to be a man anymore.[33]

Michael left academia and threw himself into the tumult of the movement. He began several organizations in the Bay Area and was one of the founders of the Gay Sunshine collective. He lived in several gay male collectives and struggled frequently to have his needs met by them. It was during this time that a sense of doom began creeping into his writings. In "An Open Letter to Tennessee Williams" (November, 1971), he wrote:

> You also taught me a sense of acceptance and resignation. Because you also taught that my fate was unavoidable, that because the source of my humanity lies in the endurance of my victimization, the price of my humanity is my submission to the strong and soulless, the men . . . I will not accept that I must submit. I will not accept that I am doomed. I will not destroy myself . . . They are making you kill yourself, as they have made generations of gay men. the best of us, kill ourselves.[34]

Michael's desperation increased. He was short on money and sold some of his possessions. He applied for welfare, borrowed money from friends. He began to write term papers for students. As he ran from the desperation, it grew beyond his control. In "The Politics of My Sex Life" (1972), Michael wrote: "I can't hide the desperation anymore and it frightens people off. And the desperation of my friends scares me . . . I'm fighting for my life because I know this society doesn't offer me a life worth living."[35] And then, one day, it became too much for him. In a short story written by Silverstein's friend Larry Tate, Michael's attempt at suicide is described:

> Michael had driven into the wooded country late at night, turned off on a little dirt road, stopped the car, left it idling, taken the length of hose and fitted one end to the exhaust, put the other end in the nearly rolled up window, stuffed a jacket in the opening by the hose. Then he had lain down on the seat. The gas had poured in. He had been almost asleep when a woman had knocked at the window, then opened the door and reached in and stopped the engine. Later he found out that the dirt road was her driveway; she had heard the car and come to investigate.[36]

Michael was taken to a psychiatric hospital for observation and then released. He spent the next five years in a series of communal houses and in increasingly radical gay organizations. Tate described this period of Michael's life as a "scrambling," but eventually he was able to find a counseling job with a gay service group, lose some weight, and begin to enter into affairs again with men.

He became involved in political organizations with a more strictly Marxist-Leninist base. Shortly before his death, Michael wrote a letter to Vince de Luca, an activist friend from his days with Berkeley's Gay Men's Rap group, that announced his departure from gay left politics because they were "white supremacist and male supremacist" and that he was "moving toward membership in a general anti-imperialist Marxist-Leninist organization in which, De Luca writes, "the gay element was submerged and which involved 'intense self-criticism.'"[37]

The June 28th Union, a radical gay group which Michael had been very active in, had broken up recently and he was left upset and angry. A few months before his suicide, Michael wrote:

> I believed it was the fact of gayness that set me apart from other white middle class men, and led me to radical politics; for me this was true. But the strength of my own feelings led me to believe that the same must be true for most other gay men. If they could only be shown how society oppressed them for being queers they would have to understand that they must take their stand on the side of all oppressed people against our common oppressors.
>
> The greatest single disillusionment of the last few years is being forced to admit that this just isn't true. Not all gay men even feel the kind of pain I felt. Fewer connect that to masculine roles or see the need to change such roles. And fewer still see such roles as part of capitalist society that can only be changed through a struggle for socialism.[38]

It was shortly after he wrote this, at a time *not* extremely different than his previous seven years, that Michael drove his car to a remote spot in Marin County, ran a hose from the exhaust pipe into the window, and asphyxiated himself. The coroner's report described his head on the seat and under the steering wheel and his feet on the passenger's side. "Bloody fluid" and "lividity" came from his nose. An off-duty policeman found him late on Saturday afternoon on February 12, 1977. Michael Silverstein was dead at the age of 36.

Several suicide notes were left, all stating similar feelings: "Help isn't what I want now. I've decided it's alright to stop if I want to. *I'm tired.*"[39]

The lives and deaths of Michael Silverstein and Claudia Scott show that, despite the best intentions of the gay movement in proclaiming "gay is good," life as a lesbian or gay man remains a difficult and, occasionally, overwhelmingly painful experience. Despite the sophisticated consciousness and political awareness that this woman and man were able to achieve, on a deeper level both Michael and Claudia were struggling with self-images that were filled with conflict and insecurity. While many people will assert that the negative self-concepts many lesbians and gay men retain are linked directly to their homosexuality, it appears obvious that homosexuality itself is not the problem, but rather it is the way in which society-at-large perceives and reacts to homosexuality. The struggle to survive as a lesbian or gay man in our society is not easy work: it puts tremendous demands on ordinary human beings. Those who cannot continue the struggle and end their own lives, like Michael and Claudia, are victims of a system which makes the lives of lesbians and gay men extremely difficult.[40]

Both Michael Silverstein and Claudia Scott came to the gay community as individuals who had tremendous personal needs. Both appear to have been unhappy people who felt isolated and alienated from other people, yet looked to a community of lesbians and gay men to provide them with the sense of belonging and integration that they needed. Claudia seemed to focus her needs specifically on individual women who would support her with unconditional love and infuse her life with meaning and direction. Michael's needs appeared to be more diffuse and included validation from the larger gay community of his personal struggle around issues of masculinity and his political ideals. While both Claudia and Michael found many valuable people in their communities, neither was able to satisfy their most basic and pressing emotional needs.

It is easy for people to fault the community for not "taking care of its own" or for failing to satisfy Michael and Claudia, yet their suicides point neither to a failure in the lesbian and gay male community nor to the failure of individual lesbians or gay men.[41] Michael and Claudia were seeking things that no community or individual could give them. They were looking to the community to provide their lives with a significance and purpose which each of us must develop on our own. The community can function as the *focus* of one's political commitment or can be the *context* within which one finds purpose and direction, but it cannot in itself charge one's life with meaning. Claudia's failure to achieve this on her own should not be seen as the failure of her community or her friends and lovers. When we look toward others to give our lives purpose, we are avoiding issues within ourselves which must be addressed through professional counseling.

It is not unusual, however, for lesbians and gay men to bring to their "coming out" tremendous expectations. Because many of us have repressed our emotional and sexual feelings for long periods of time, we expect that, once we are free of the self-repression, all our personal tensions and problems will drop away. In our enthusiasm in urging others to come out as lesbians and gay men, we often tend to ignore or minimize the hazards and difficulties of openly gay lives. Admitting that the coming out process includes pitfalls and painful times does not mean that we are proclaiming it an unwise move for closeted homosexuals. It means, however, that we are aware of the risks involved and encourage women and men to proceed through the process at their own rates and schedules. Furthermore, as a community we must become aware that people who have just come out are subject to mood swings, regrets and fears, and inner conflicts. Community programs to help people through their entrance into their identities as lesbians and gay men are greatly needed.

Many local communities do provide discussion groups and counseling programs for gay people who have recently come out. These groups tend to perform several functions. They provide an individual with access to information about the community (what organizations, activities, clubs, services are available) as well as a space to share their feelings with other women or men who are also new to the community. An unfortunate tendency of these groups, however, is to spur an individual into more active and open participation in the community before they are emotionally prepared for such experiences. This may be brought about by a well-intentioned group leader who feels that her or his role is to inspire others to leap from the closet in a grand way or by other members of the group who present more subtle pressure that leaves the impression that the more open and public one is about one's sexuality the "better" one is as a person and community member. It is essential that we recognize that many people need to make a gradual transition into their identities as lesbians or gay men and that any attempt to rush them, however well-intentioned, may ultimately prove harmful.

The greatest danger lies in the ignorance most people maintain about the practical life experiences involved in living as a lesbian or gay man in our culture. While many people anticipate all kinds of problems involved in interfacing with their "nongay" lives after they come out, they believe that their "gay lives" will be trouble-free. This often results in conflicting feelings which arise during the initial period of identification as a gay person. As much as the joy of being able to acknowledge one's honest attraction and love for others of one's sex is an uplifting experience, the new problems and conflicts which one is confronted with can be overwhelming. If one has anticipated gay life to be filled with perfect orgasms and fairy-tale romances, one may be quite disappointed. The realization that the lesbian and gay community is comprised of real people with real qualities as well as real flaws comes as a surprise to many. Helping lesbians and gay men through this disconcerting and painful time must be a priority for us as individuals and for our community.

Such help and support were not enough for Michael and Claudia. They came to the community with deeper problems and pains than any individual or rap group could contend with. Claudia's journals show that her feelings of alienation and isolation go well beyond her identity as a lesbian and that what she truly needed was help from people trained and experienced in psychological matters. Michael's self-hatred and intense anger had no simple solutions either. The tremendous irony of his situation was that his ability to be aware of the sources of his self-hatred in societal homophobia, sexism and anti-Semitism did not allow him to break out of his cycle of victimization. Despite his intellectual pledge "I will not accept that I am doomed," Michael needed tremendous support to continue living.

Many people also assume that once a lesbian or gay man has been functioning in the community for a long period of time, and particularly if they have been politically active, the risk of depression and regret disappears. We have no studies to indicate that politically active lesbians and gay men are any healthier or more psychologically stable than nonpolitically active community members. The suicides of activists in the community include Don Miller, who was president of the Gay Student Union at California State College in Fullerton; Jan Sergienko, a woman writer of *Philadelphia Gay News*; and Terry Mangan, a gay historian and member of the Denver Gay Coalition.[42] The assumption that activism defeats one's personal conflicts, however, has allowed many activists to deny their inner turmoil and feel that, merely by assuming the role of activist, they achieve new vistas in mental health. Statements by writers who seem to agree with this assumption do not help the matter:

> Suicide is the ultimate violence to oneself. It is the most extreme reaction to guilt, a final solution. The machinations of guilt take over the personality and mete out a punishment more severe even than society would wish. Can heterosexual society comprehend the agony a Lesbian has gone through who conceives of death as the only solution?
>
> Every Lesbian knows of women who have taken this final route out beyond their peripheral and despised position in society to nothingness. Gay women may attempt suicide as a desperate cry for help. Emotional and psychological pressures have become too much to bear alone. They may have tried to ask their parents to hear them and may have paid a professional listener (therapist),

and still felt they were not heard. Instead of destroying unjust laws and attitudes, they destroy themselves. Alone they feel helpless and fear life more than death.

The suicide's anger turns upon herself; a Lesbian activist's turns outward. Both are saying: "I cannot and will not live any other way, and I cannot live my way the way things are now."[43]

The assumption that we either turn our anger inwards or outwards ignores those of us who do both. The work of activists today involves changing both their society and their selves.

It is important to note here that the deaths of lesbian and gay male activists—regardless of the circumstances surrounding them—are frequently immediately considered to be suicides by medical examiners and police authorities. This is particularly interesting because under normal (read "heterosexual") circumstances, authorities are reluctant to consider a death a suicide unless a note has been found, until an appropriate autopsy report has been released and the friends and relatives of the deceased provide evidence to support such a conclusion. Authorities have also been known to favor the wishes of the families who hope to disguise the suicide and "protect the family name."

When Margo Karle, a prominent New York lesbian attorney active in lesbian and gay rights cases, was found shot in the head in her home in Eastern Long Island, Police Detective Richard Zito insisted he was not able to conclude whether Karle's death was an accident, murder or suicide. Despite this assertion, Zito commented, "Everyone that's associated with her that I've spoken to has been less than candid. I think they're protecting her ... by giving only positive sides. But I've never seen this done to this degree before, and I've been doing this work for years. It's almost like there's a campaign on to view this as an accident, if you see what I'm getting at. But this doesn't help an investigation. What helps is to know what a person was thinking, what kind of stress they were under ... Sometimes fighting all those causes can get to be burdensome."[44]

The death of David Brill, political writer for *Gay Community News* in Boston, merits a detailed investigation. Twenty-five year old Brill was found dead in his bedroom at his family's house in Winthrop, Massachusetts, on November 15, 1979.[45] Within hours—with no autopsy report, no substantial clues, and no substantial interviews with friends and family—local police were calling the death "a probable suicide."[46] The autopsy, which later showed that Brill died of cyanide poisoning, allowed the mainstream press and medical authorities (along with too many members of Boston's gay community) to conclude within days of the death that Brill had committed suicide. The only substantial investigations into his death were supposedly spearheaded by police officials. An investigation by the local gay community or by *Gay Community News* never materialized. Thus it was almost six months after Brill's death, when the *Boston Globe Magazine* ran a major article on the death, that many friends and colleagues learned that the container of cyanide rumored to have been found next to Brill's body—was actually found in the basement of his house—four flights away.[47] Furthermore, no glass or small vial was found in Brill's room. Since it is impossible to ingest a swig of cyanide and then run up four flights of stairs and through several doors, it became clear that suspicious circumstances surrounded this death. Furthermore, Brill's treasured appointment book had vanished from his house. Despite the dangerous investigative work Brill was involved in and the regular threats on his life, most people easily believed that the heavy-set, Jewish gay boy killed himself. With their characteristic lack of competence in such cases, the police allowed the case to be closed and recorded as a suicide. Again one wonders whether such shoddy investigations and abuses of procedure by the authorities would have occurred had Brill not been homosexual and had not been an activist.

A significant aspect of Claudia Scott's suicide is that it occurred during the Christmas holiday and Claudia was aware of the risks the season held for her. There are conflicting studies concerning whether or not more people commit suicide during holidays, particularly the period between Thanksgiving, Christmas and New Years. Experts agree, however, that people are more likely to recognize feelings of isolation, loneliness and unhappiness during a period when many people are publicly celebrating with friends and loved ones.

For a lesbian or gay man, holidays can be extremely difficult times. Since many gay people are estranged from their families or have deliberately distanced themselves from parents and siblings, traditional holidays can heighten their awareness of being "different." A group of friends or a lover can certainly be good substitutes for one's natural family, but finding oneself alone during a holiday can be a deeply depressing experience.

A staffer from the Samaritans in Boston, a suicide-prevention hotline, reported that on one Christmas Day the first eight calls she received on the shift were from gay men who had spent the entire day in bars and were lonely, depressed and desperate.[48] A lesbian who had been suicidal for a long period of time said, "It was on the first Christmas Eve that I was no longer with my lover that I realized how unhappy I had been since we broke up. Not having the holidays with her made me very depressed and, for the first time, I consciously thought about ending it all."[49]

How much of this kind of thinking was involved with Claudia's suicide is impossible to say. It is clear from her journal, however, that the holidays brought on an awareness that her relationship with Frances was definitely different than it had been when they were lovers and that this awareness was deeply painful and disappointing to her.

As a community, lesbians and gay men need to develop alternative ways of celebrating holidays in order to make sure that those of us who are not involved in a romantic relationship or in a friendship or family network feel supported during these periods. Community dinners and activities that stress the incorporation of new people into the community may be particularly helpful. It is also important for each of us to be aware of our friends during a holiday season and make sure the ones who are feeling particularly lonely or isolated are cared for. By incorporating these people into our plans, we may help them enjoy an otherwise difficult season.

Claudia and Michael's suicides exhibit a basic distinction between the ways women and men respond to feelings of depression and anger. Both of these people were writers and somewhat public figures in their communities. Michael's anger was expressed publicly, in what he said and in what he wrote. He developed a reputation as an angry and depressed man. Claudia, on the other hand, appeared to be a stable and reliable person in the lesbian community and her public writings did not reveal the pain and depression that she felt. Only in her private journals did she express these feelings.

While stereotypes of the sexes lead us to believe that women indulge their feelings and men keep their feelings hidden from public view, it is apparent that men have more societally approved ways of dealing with specific feelings, including anger, than women have. Men are expected to turn their anger outward, express it in speeches and in writing, bring it into their relations with other people, force it onto their families. Women are expected to direct their anger inwards and deal with it privately. Lesbian writer Adrienne Rich has written about this concerning poet Anne Sexton:

> We have had enough suicidal women poets, enough suicidal women, enough of self-destructiveness as the sole form of violence permitted to women.

I would like to list, in Anne's honor and memory, some of the ways in which we destroy ourselves. Self-trivialization is one. Believing the lie that women are not capable of major creations. Not taking ourselves or our work seriously enough; always finding the needs of others more demanding than our own. Being content to produce intellectual or artistic work in which we imitate men . . . When we begin to feel compassion for ourselves and each other, instead of for our rapists, we will begin to be immune to suicide . . .[50]

This is not to say that all lesbians who commit suicide follow Claudia's pattern or that all suicides of gay men share Michael's public unleashing of his anger and pain. Regardless of the fact that lesbians and gay men share a sexual orientation toward other women or other men, lesbians are women and gay men are men. We tend to exhibit much the same psychological patterns that others of our sex exhibit. Claudia's suicide, complete with her public facade of propriety and stability, is similar to the suicides of many women. Anger and pain, rightfully directed outwards, is here forced inward, with tragic results.

The suicides of Claudia Scott and Michael Silverstein make clear the efforts that must be made by many lesbians and gay men to stay alive. With the tremendous burden which our culture puts upon people who are "different" from the white, straight, middle-class man, it is remarkable that so many people who are "different" are able to stay alive. As gay writer Charley Shively wrote concerning the suicides of gay men, the question should not be "Why did he do it?" but "How did he hold out as long as he did?"[51]

5.

Substance Abuse and Gay Suicide

"Self-trivialization, contempt for women, misplaced compassion, addiction; if we could purge ourselves of this quadruple poison, we would have minds and bodies more poised for the act of survival and rebuilding."
—Adrienne Rich, from "Anne Sexton: 1928–1974"

Substance abuse has consistently been linked to increased risk of suicide in the general population. Counselors who work at suicide prevention agencies report a strong correlation between suicide attempts and alcohol and drug abuse among the lesbian and gay male population. Valerie Waidler of San Francisco's Suicide Prevention, Inc., said, "Particularly for the male homosexual, I think we see a very high frequency of alcohol use and the use of other drugs among depressed callers. We're seeing people trying to cope with loss and depression through drinking and through drugs."[1] For an article titled "Alcohol Abuse Among Lesbians," Deborah L. Diamond and Sharon C. Wilsnack did intensive personal interviews with ten lesbians who had drinking problems. All women in the study drank in response to feelings of depression. Seven of the ten women had experienced thoughts about suicide and four had made attempts.[2]

As with suicide statistics, statistics on alcoholism vary greatly depending on how the researchers are defining certain key terms, the procedures used to determine an individual's alcoholism or abuse of alcohol, and the sampling obtained of the population. It appears evident, however, that lesbians and gay men are at much greater risk than the heterosexual population for alcohol abuse and alcoholism. Approximately 30% of both the lesbian and gay male populations have problems with alcoholism.[3] One study of gay men found that 29.4% of the men interviewed reported "drinking more than they should . . . nearly all the time."[4] Another study found that 30% of the male homosexuals sampled were problem drinkers while only 20% of the heterosexual control group shared similar status.[5] A study which compared a group of lesbians with a group of unmarried heterosexual women discovered that 35% of the lesbians experienced alcohol abuse while only 5% of the heterosexual women had similar problems.[6]

A survey taken of gay men in four urban centers in Kansas found that one-third of the men were alcoholics, and a similar study done by the Gay Community Services Center in Los Angeles found that 10% of the gay population of the city was at a "crisis" stage of alcoholism and an additional 21% of the population was at "high risk." This study showed that between 25% and 35% of the lesbian community in Los Angeles had problems with alcoholism.[7]

Reasons for the high degree of alcoholism in the lesbian and gay community include the pivotal role that bars play in the lives of lesbians and gay men, the frequent resort to alcohol and substance abuse to deal with societal oppression, and the importance alcohol plays in the social networks of many lesbians and gay men. Alcoholism is a problem for a large number of gay people and is linked in case after case to depression and suicidal ideation.

One lesbian described her relationship with alcohol abuse:

> Once I got into the bars I never got off the stool. This was when I was just coming out. I needed to identify; therefore, I thought that I had to go to bars, drink and dress a certain way—and this was what being gay was. By the time that I had caught myself I found that I just liked to drink, and it has nothing to do with being gay. I had juxtaposed various associations with homosexuality— being depressed and being alcoholic. In other words I was carrying out a script that I had written in my head—I didn't like gayness, I didn't feel that I had made any choices about my life until I stopped drinking. For all that I was feeling, I drink and I was gay, a sick association that I had projected. Having to socialize in a bar helped me along in a drinking habit. I became addicted to the bar itself and it got so that I didn't want to go anywhere if I didn't know that there was going to be booze there. I didn't make a social life outside of the bar—I stayed in my lonely corner, liked it there and liked being miserable. Before I realized that I was not in control others had to make choices for me. I now realize that I had emotional problems that I had to straighten out regardless of whether I was straight or gay.[8]

This statement reveals typical patterns for many lesbians and gay men: the association of their sexuality with alcoholism, the dependence on bars, the inability of many people to deal with the conflicts surrounding their homosexuality. The experiences of lesbians and gay men provide the clearest examples of how alcohol is linked to feelings of self-destructiveness. The inability of the traditional networks which people use to support their recovery from alcoholism—family, church, school, employers—are closed to many gay people. Bill's story, recounted below, illustrates the importance of developing alternatives for gay alcoholics.

Bill arrived at an awareness of his homosexuality one day when he was in the gym locker room of his high school. After spending a typically male early adolescence playing locker room games, snapping towels and goosing other boys, at 15 Bill realized that he seemed to derive more pleasure out of his contact with boys than did most of his peers. "The realization happened one day when I was closing the door of my locker," Bill recalled. "I had spent a few minutes running around the locker room, goosing guys, and all of a sudden I said to myself, 'You know, Bill, you really like men.' My next thought was, 'I must be queer!'"[9]

Bill's realization was accompanied by strong feelings of guilt, confusion and fear. He traces these feelings to his strict Catholic upbringing. The only information that he had about homosexuality was that it was morally wrong. The only homosexuals that he knew about were "the grungy queers who hung out at the bus station." Bill decided that such a life was not for him. He would do his best to keep his homosexuality under strict control.

During the next two years Bill battled with strong feelings of guilt. He frequently masturbated, which he knew the church considered a mortal sin, but this was the only means he had of exercising his sexuality, since direct contact with another man was more sinful. At the age of 17, Bill had his first sexual experience with another male. He remembers the incident as "quick and sleazy"—he was fellated by a man in the men's room of a neighborhood cinema. After returning home from the movie, Bill confided in a younger cousin his fears that he must be "queer"; he trusted her because she had a reputation for being socially aware and "cool" on issues of sex and sexuality. He also told her that if he were, in fact, homosexual, it "would be better for me to kill myself, than to drag others along to hell with me."

This threat of suicide worried his cousin, and she went to her mother with the information, who in turn told her husband, who was Bill's uncle. Thus Bill's father received the word that his son was both "queer" and intent on suicide. As a child, Bill had been a slow

grower and a late talker, and Bill's father assumed that Bill's homosexual feelings were signs that he was sexually "slow," also. Since Bill
had been "slow" all his life, his father had expected to hear about
this kind of "homosexual playing-around" when Bill was 15 or 16;
he saw homosexuality as merely a phase that his son would grow out
of.

Bill soon graduated from high school and continued his education
at a monastery school; after his first month, Bill confided to a priest
that he thought he was a homosexual. Within three days, Bill found
himself discharged from the monastery and on his way home. His
parents had been informed by the priest, and though they had no
reason to panic because this was not news to them, they were concerned about Bill's future and, particularly, about his education.

Next Bill was sent off to a state college in upstate New York. His
early college days were filled with confusion and turmoil. Bill was
sexually active, but his experiences were "very quick ten-minute
things" and not the romance that filled his fantasies. Sexual encounters left him feeling guilty, and he often went directly from sex
to the priest for confession. The fraternity he lived in was generally
unsupportive, and he seems to have been recognized from the start
as being homosexual. "I'm the kind of person," Bill said, "who, if
you're aware of homosexuality, you can tell I'm gay right away." At
the fraternity, "People were talking about me, making fun of me,
but not always to my face," he said. These were daily incidents in
Bill's life at the age of 18. This is also the time during which Bill
began to have a drinking problem.

The first time Bill "went drinking" was on his first day of college.
He remembers hoping to find acceptance and approval from his
classmates by getting very drunk. This first experience was also his
first alcoholic blackout, and he remembers nothing that happened
after the drinking began. Blackouts would become a pattern in Bill's
drinking over the next ten years.

In 1965, when Bill was 19, he met Gabriel, then 27, at a bar near
campus and formed a relationship that lasted for a year and a half.
Gabriel was the first gay man that Bill had known intimately for any
length of time, and Bill quickly developed strong feelings of respect
and love for him. "To me," Bill recalls, "Gabriel had it all together.
He pursued all his interests, including his interest in men, free from
guilt." While Gabriel was certainly not as open about his homosexuality as many gay men have become in recent years, he was
comfortable enough with it to neither flaunt nor deny it, and this
impressed Bill very much. Bill was further intrigued by Gabriel

because the man had recently left the Catholic Church and become an Anglican.

A week after they met and before they became intensely involved, Bill and Gabriel had arranged to meet and spend the evening together. Bill arrived early at the bar they had agreed to meet in and had a few drinks to "relax" himself. When Gabriel entered the bar he walked right past Bill, ignoring him. A few minutes later, the bartender came over to Bill and told him, in threatening tones, to stay away from Gabriel. When Bill asked for an explanation, he was told, "Because he's mine." Bill walked over to Gabriel for confirmation, and Gabriel told him that this was true. Bill left the bar angry, depressed and inebriated.

Once out on the street Bill panicked. He went to a telephone, called his priest, and immediately went to see him. The priest told Bill, "This is God's way of telling you that you should not be with this man." Bill received no comfort from these words, and he went back to another bar in town and drank heavily. By midnight he was very drunk and his feelings of sadness and anger overcame him. Overwhelmed by desperation, he walked out of the bar, off the curb, and deliberately stepped in front of an oncoming car.

The automobile did not hit him. The next thing Bill remembers is being surrounded by angry police officers who took him to headquarters and charged him with drunk and disorderly conduct. They asked him why he had tried to kill himself, and Bill answered directly, "Because I'm queer." Realizing that they had a difficult situation on their hands, the officers called in the dean of students, who had a reputation for being a "high moralist"; but rather than talk with him, Bill immediately asked the dean to call in his priest. The priest came to the stationhouse and arranged for all the charges to be dropped, on the condition that Bill begin psychotherapy immediately.

Bill was in counseling for the next nine months with a private psychologist; at the same time he developed his relationship with Gabriel. He found much of the counseling to be boring and manipulative, but he was fortunate to be placed with a therapist with some degree of sensitivity to gay people. Bill's parents met with the doctor to make sure that Bill would be made into a heterosexual through the therapy process. The counselor said adamantly that Bill would have to decide whether he wanted to be gay or straight, not his parents.

While counseling did have some positive effects on Bill, it did not make him a stable person, and it did not make him happy about his attraction to men. The year and a half that Bill spent with Gabriel was romantic, and Bill remembers regular lunches with him on campus and infrequent but satisfying sex. Gabriel took on a paternal role with Bill and always told Bill that he loved him, rather than that he was *in* love with him. The distinction was felt deeply by Bill. The relationship, however, was marred by Bill's erratic behavior and his regular periods of drunkenness. Bill flunked out of college at this time and went to work, first as a waiter and then at a local radio station.

One night when Bill showed up at Gabriel's home, Gabriel told him that the relationship was over. Gabriel did not give a full explanation of the reasons, but Bill heard the finality in his tone and left, brokenhearted and stunned. It was not until almost a year later that Bill found out that Gabriel had cut all his friends off at this time because he was dying of leukemia.

Bill blamed himself for the breakup and reacted with depression, a wild drinking spree, and another suicide attempt. He decided to move to Troy, New York, a small city adjacent to Albany, because he wanted to be in a larger gay community and he had some friends in that town. It was shortly after this move, and while he was on the rebound from Gabriel, that Bill met his next lover, Michael.

Michael was 25, five years older than Bill. He was tall, dark and aggressive and Bill was immediately attracted to him. Michael shared Bill's history of depression and also had a history of suicide attempts. He had been living with older gay men since he was 14 and the men had provided for all of Michael's needs. Recently he had graduated from college and was living with a physician outside Albany. Their relationship was tumultuous because of Michael's disinterest in his partner and his own alcoholism; the men fought frequently.

In assessing Michael's alcoholism, Bill believes that homosexuality was not a major causal factor; rather that he was wracked by conflict caused by his dependence on older men. While Michael often expressed the desire to make a break with his doctor friend and lead an independent life, his dependence kept him from making the break. The conflict surrounding this issue made Michael very confused and, at times, desperate.

Michael and Bill were friends and lovers for six months. Bill was aware of how Michael was tortured by his dependence on his doctor friend and by his own lack of motivation. While Michael seemed to be free from many of Bill's own tendencies towards guilt and anguish over his homosexuality, Michael's anxiety came from his extremely romantic notions of life and his desire to imitate a heterosexual relationship and play the "housewife" role. Michael's relationship with his doctor friend became increasingly intolerable as Michael became more involved with Bill. The doctor struck Michael at times, which increased Michael's feelings of helplessness and frustration. He began to talk with Bill about his desires to "get out of this life." Claiming that no one would mourn his passing, Michael confided that he found life so intolerable that he would not last much longer. While Bill tried to comfort and support his friend, it became clear to him that Michael's needs were insurmountable.

On one of the last nights of his life, Michael drove Bill to work and said goodbye to him. Bill remembers, "I knew what he was saying when he said goodbye. I knew what he was going to do. I wanted to reach over and kiss him and I didn't because there were all these other people around. I pleaded with him to call me after the weekend and he said that he would, but I knew what was going to happen and I knew there was nothing I could do about it."

This was Friday night and Michael killed himself on Sunday morning. Michael buried his face in ether-soaked material and put a plastic bag around his head. He went to sleep and died, leaving no note. Bill believes that Michael deliberately tried to make his suicide appear as if the doctor had murdered him.

Bill was not told about the death for a month. He tried to get information from Michael's family and from his doctor-lover, but no one told him the truth. Michael's family quickly buried the body in a Catholic funeral and notified none of Michael's gay friends. They initially told Bill that their son had "moved" and that he had left no forwarding address or phone number. Since Michael had been toying with the idea of moving to Massachusetts, Bill wanted to believe the story, yet he continued to call the family frequently for more information. Finally, Bill was able to contact Michael's father who again insisted that Michael had moved. Bill confronted him and the man asked, "Are you the boy from Troy?" When Bill answered that he was, Michael's father replied, "I'm sorry then, but Michael is not all right. He is dead."

Bill was at work at the time in a hospital as an orderly. When he got off the phone he was very upset and told his supervisor that his "best friend" had died. The man was unsympathetic and hostile and said that it was clear that Bill would be no use to the hospital that day. Bill had much difficulty dealing with his grief because he could not tell his co-workers the full nature of his relationship with Michael. The usual channels of grieving were closed to him.

Instead Bill threw himself into his work, working extra shifts and overtime. He went on another alcoholic binge and spent several months drinking excessively. During this time he also learned that Gabriel had died and his feelings of fatality and despair were overwhelming. Bill recalled, "I had to protect myself, because I had so much to deal with. First dealing with Michael's death and then Gabe's on top of it. It was too much for me." The following six months were spent in a self-imposed mourning. Friends would encourage Bill to join them at parties and events, but he would refuse.

These deaths had a profound effect on Bill's self-image and his feelings about being gay. He had been moving towards a more militant attitude about his homosexuality since the night he met Michael. They had met at the Shangrila, a gay bar in Albany, in October, 1967. Because it was an election year, the police were "cleaning up the town." Four straight men came into the bar and began punching the gay patrons and throwing furniture and smashing bottles. Bill became enraged and started yelling, "There's four of them and four hundred of us" and urged a resistance. He was quickly arrested for drunk and disorderly conduct ("One of the rare nights when I wasn't") and spent the night in jail. Bill's rage concerning this incident and the general mistreatment of gay people made him decide that "It was time for gay people to fight back." With Michael and Gabriel's deaths, he began to express his anger overtly and regularly incited hostile attacks on straight men who were harassing gay men near bars or on the streets. His anger had turned into violent activity.

The deaths also affected Bill's attitudes about relationships. "I realized at this time," Bill said, "that all relationships end—with divorce, split-up, or death. Each person has to have a life of their own, because eventually you'll be left alone and, hopefully, you'll be able to stand on your own two feet."

Bill felt the need to change his life and his surroundings. Life in Troy held too many painful memories and he was becoming increasingly obsessed with the deaths of his two lovers. Michael and Bill had often talked about moving from the Albany area and their favorite fantasy destination was Boston. In January, 1969, Bill packed his few belongings, got on a Greyhound bus, and moved to Boston. He found a job in a tie factory and settled into an apartment.

The next year was difficult for him. His alcoholism became more severe and the suicide attempts began again. He made half-hearted attempts at death by asphyxiation and pills. While Bill feels the attempts began as a "cry for help," they soon grew more destructive.

He began to mix drugs and alcohol and suffered frequent blackouts, several lasting for many days.

One night when Bill was feeling particularly lonely and depressed, he went to a local bar, the Punch Bowl. He was chatting with a man he had just met when he realized that it was April 5, the anniversary of Michael's death. In a stupor of alcohol and remorse, Bill went into the bathroom, smashed a beer bottle, and jabbed his wrists. At first people did not realize what he had done. He was soon found by a friend, however, and taken to the hospital where his wounds were stitched up.

Bill's extreme alcoholism and suicide attempts continued over the next five years. Much of what happened during this period Bill cannot remember. He found work as an orderly in a hospital and entered a training program as an ophthalmic technician. He spent his weekends drunk in any number of local bars and only sobered up to come to work on Monday. On several occasions he was too sick to work and he finally had to leave his job because of his frequent absences.

In 1970 Bill met Bob, another man who became his first long-term lover since Michael. Bill frequently compared the two men, causing great tensions in the relationship. Bill moved in with Bob and the men lived together for a year and a half. While Bob was not alcoholic, he did have strong, ambivalent feelings about being gay and he also had difficulty dealing with Bill's alcoholic binges and suicide attempts.

On Bill's 25th birthday, the men had a party at their home. Bill had been feeling depressed because Michael had said, shortly before he died, that life goes downhill after 25, which led Bill to tell himself that perhaps "it is wiser to leave when life is good." Since Bill saw Bob paying attention to another man, he used this excuse to go into their bathroom in the middle of the party and take all the pills that were in the medicine cabinet. Bob reacted to the suicide attempt with panic and disgust and shortly afterwards they broke up. Bill lived alone, retreating into his alcoholic trance for a year and then moved to Cape Cod.

On the Cape, Bill got a job at a hospital but again lost it because of his frequent absences brought on by drinking. This dismissal from his job made him very depressed and the next year was very difficult for him. It was made even more difficult because he had moved in with Donald, a 24 year old man who had no employment interest and was satisfied to stay home and clean and cook. He was also a liar and he toyed with Bill in dangerous ways. He told Bill that he was visiting doctors in New York when he was really going there to meet other men. One time he told Bill that he was seriously ill and needed the heart surgery he was refusing to have. He told Bill that the doctors predicted he'd live another year without the operation and, before the year was over, he was planning to get in his car and drive off a bluff into the sea.

This set off a powerful reaction in Bill. He connected Donald's doom with Michael's and Gabriel's deaths and was overwhelmed to see this happening again to someone he was close to. As Donald dramatized his supposed fate, Bill became more and more depressed until one day he made another attempt at suicide by getting drunk and swallowing Quaaludes and Valium. He boarded a bus for Boston, where he went to a bar, drank some more and took more pills. At this time he became extremely dizzy and his vision began to have a tunnel effect—everyone seemed to be at the end of a long tunnel. The visual impairment made Bill panic and he realized that he could actually die from the combination of pills and liquor. He immediately went to a nearby hospital.

At this city hospital he was interviewed by a psychiatric nurse who told him he could not have sincerely wanted to kill himself because he still had pills left in his pocket. Bill swiftly left the hospital and hailed a cab for a state hospital. By this time he had become quite confused and ill. The cab driver took him to the emergency room and the attending doctor admitted him to the hospital for a ten-day stay where he could rest and be observed.

Bill's stay in the psychiatric unit was not pleasant. He was harassed by doctors who pressed him for information about his sexuality that he found inappropriate ("Why do you see yourself as a woman?"), yet failed to ask about his history of alcohol and drug abuse. The stay had a positive effect on him, however. By the time he left he realized that he was saner and more in control of himself than he had thought. He also realized how easy it was for a person to be involuntarily institutionalized and he was afraid that this might happen to him. He decided that he never wanted to find himself as a psychiatric inpatient again.

The decision to avoid hospitalization, however, was not enough to cure Bill's acute alcoholism. After his release he found a job with a real estate firm. Four months later he was caught embezzling money to support his drinking habit. He was fired by his employer who had the police issue a warrant for his arrest.

This was a difficult time for Bill. He fled his apartment and spent days sleeping on the Esplanade, a public park on Boston's Charles

River, or staying in friends' apartments. After running out of money, he was sent $25 by his father, but he cashed the check at a local bar and drank all night. The next morning when he awoke he found a mere $1.50 in his pockets. This made him realize that the drinking was out of control.

Once again Bill found himself in a serious situation and he finally decided that he had to do something about his alcoholism. He attended his first Alcoholics Anonymous meeting, a major step toward admitting he had a problem. During the next three months he became sober and avoided all alcohol.

Just when Bill was reaching a stable point, he became ill and was admitted to a hospital. The doctor's initial diagnosis was that Bill had cancer and would need a colostomy. While he later found out that he was suffering from nonspecific proctitis, a much less serious condition, the shock of being told he might have cancer brought Bill back to the panic state. "I had just started to enjoy life," Bill recalled. "Now I was being told I had to face death." This started the drinking again. Bill stopped eating and became ill as his weight dropped.

Bill spent much of the next month in an alcoholic blackout. He went to visit Michael's grave near Albany and was feeling dangerously desperate again. He flirted with attending AA meetings but lacked any ability to work regularly with the organization. A friend arranged for Bill to go on welfare and, at the same time, encouraged him strongly to stay sober. Bill found a job caring for an elderly doctor who had recently had a stroke.

It is difficult to explain definitively what combination of factors allowed Bill to pull himself out of his long-term pattern of alcoholism and self-destructive behavior at this time. His new job placed him in supportive surroundings and gave him a structured and clearly-defined life. His work was demanding and brought him into the doctor's family, which included several health professionals who supported Bill in his move towards sobriety. In March, 1975, Bill stopped drinking altogether and began working very closely with the AA program. A year later he became involved with a local suicide-prevention agency and began helping others who had been suicidal. Bill found that, by becoming involved in the agency, in AA and in his new "family," he became strong enough to fight his dependence on booze. Bill's new "family" had no difficulty with his homosexuality. They saw his drinking problem as a drinking problem.

Bill's story seems like a typical success story from this point forward. While he fought against occasional relapses, Bill was finally successful in becoming sober and energetically worked to help other alcoholics. He formed several relationships with men that were neither as desperate nor intense as his earlier relationships because his needs were no longer as great. By developing a community and a family of his own, Bill was able to feel supported by many people. When the elderly doctor died, Bill was left a legacy to use for nursing school and found nursing to be work that he did very well. At the present time, Bill is sober, happier and involved in a five-year, stable relationship with a man he finds wonderful, reliable and caring.

Bill's personal battle against depression and alcoholism has a happy ending, yet one cannot help but be impressed with the man's ability to pull himself out of his long-term pattern of alcohol abuse and self-destructive behavior. What is most notable is that, from the very early stages of Bill's alcoholism, the traditional support networks available to most people—family, church, school counselors, psychiatrists—insisted on seeing Bill's homosexuality as the sickness that needed to be treated rather than his depression or his alcoholism. The failure to accept Bill's homosexuality and help him develop coping techniques that would permit him to respond appropriately to societal pressures resulting from attitudes towards homosexuality resulted in Bill's constantly being placed into situations which only exacerbated the problems. It is very easy for people who have little understanding of lesbians and gay men and the problems we face to determine that suicide attempts and depression, as well as alcoholism, are the result of one's being homosexual rather than a response to the special problems gay people encounter with society.

This is most obvious with Bill's experience in the psychiatric hospital where, despite the fact that he arrived filled with pills and liquor, the doctors insisted on exploring his homosexuality and his gender identification rather than his abuse of drugs and alcohol. Lesbians and gay men have experienced increasing distrust of the medical profession as the result of decades of medical "treatment" of homosexuality. While some people may argue that it is necessary for psychiatrists to explore a gay man's feelings about his gayness if they are to treat his substance abuse problems appropriately, it appears that Bill's doctors saw his gayness *by definition* as the problem rather than the substance abuse. Bill's decision to avoid further institutionalization was perhaps the wisest personal decision aiding his recovery. Instead of relying on psychiatrists and institutions, Bill sought the support of friends who would not question his homosexuality, as well as Alcoholics Anonymous, which has become a group that is very accepting of a person's sexuality choices.

Early experiences Bill had with the deaths of close friends and lovers who were gay provide another interesting clue to his own tendency towards suicidal activity. Gabriel's early death from leukemia separated Bill inexplicably from the one gay man he had known who had seemed to deal with his homosexuality in an appropriate and healthy manner. Michael's suicide, after Bill had been involved with him for half a year, again exposed Bill to a close male friend's death. In both cases, Bill was not permitted the usual forms of grieving and mourning. Not only was he not allowed to attend either funeral, he was not even informed of either death within a reasonable time after it had occurred. This could only help to encourage Bill's tendency to become obsessive over his friends' deaths and to identify with their pain. Funeral services provide people with an appropriate setting to express their grief and find support from other people who had been close to the deceased person. Bill dealt with his grief in isolation. He was not even permitted to take time off from work because he could not explain to his employer the significance of his relationship with Michael for he would not have retained his job if he were open about being gay.

The fact that Bill was able to continue his pattern of alcohol and drug abuse for over ten years without ever receiving substantial support to remedy the situation is partially the result of his transience and his inability to establish a stable set of friends and to integrate himself into a helpful community. Once Bill was able to find a job that accepted him and his problems, he found himself among people who could support his attempt to go sober and strengthen himself. Because many gay people are often forced to leave their families and begin a life apart—in a break more decisive and uprooting than young heterosexuals who separate themselves from their families—the assumption that a natural support system exists in everyone's life is unfounded. We often find ourselves, after we have come out as gay people, without the ties to a family or an ethnic community that we enjoyed before. The reestablishment of some kind of community is essential to provide a gay person with a supportive network. Unfortunately, most of us have not been prepared to do this kind of community establishment work. Bill's relative isolation for a long period of time is indicative of his inability to successfully integrate himself into a community.

Not every gay man survives his bouts with depression, alcohol and drug abuse. Allyn Amundson was such a man. By all accounts he was remarkable and talented, an artist of great skill and creativity. He had taught painting and art history at the University of Wisconsin and Michigan State University before coming to Boston in the summer of 1963.[10] One friend describes him as a "hippie, a flower child, a dissenter long before those notions were fully part of the contemporary American conscience."[11] Another wrote, "Allyn loved being different and unique and he succeeded . . . He always wanted either to be rich or famous and since he saw that he couldn't achieve either he decided to be outrageous in personality and appearance. He was egocentric and loved being noticed if for no other reason than just being noticed . . . He loved to spur other people along life's tedious journey with grand encouragement. He was never selfish with praise even if he didn't completely understand. He was seldom a 'downer.'"[12]

Despite a personality which projected sociability and joy, Allyn had problems which he shared with few friends. Those who knew him well called him "tortured and tormented,"[13] "alone and afraid."[14] Friends worried about his drinking habits and wondered at the causes for the drinking. Shortly before Allyn's suicide, one close friend was moved to inquire about help for Allyn:

> I had talked to an alcoholic counselor earlier in the week about what a friend who respects another man's right to private destruction does when everything starts to fall apart for that friend. He said talk about it. All the friend can do is kick you the hell out. I was going to do it even though I didn't want to be kicked out.[15]

When he next saw Allyn, Allyn informed him that he'd started group therapy and that he was feeling that it was helping him. This was the last time his friend saw him alive.

Allyn had clearly decided to kill himself and he invited his close friends for a final farewell visit the week before he died. They were unaware of his decision and were shocked when they heard that, while tripping on acid, he jumped from a fourth-floor apartment window on Blossom Street in Boston, across from his favorite bar. Friends felt shocked and pained at his death. Dolores Klaich, who had dedicated her book *Woman + Woman* to Allyn as an old friend and the first gay person she ever knew, wrote:

> I'm distressed by his death; I feel a little like Colette when she heard of the poet Renée Vivien's death. Colette said, "Like all those who never use their strength to the limit, I am hostile to those who let life burn them out."

Allyn, like the poet Renée Vivien, was not a survivor. But they certainly were livers. And their legacies—Vivien's poems, yet to be translated into English, and Allyn's paintings and drawings are there to bring joy. Especially to their gay Sisters and Brothers who, against still frustrating odds, have chosen to survive, and to fight.[16]

Allyn's lover asked for a leave of absence from his job in a rural school district to recover from his grief. Explaining (as Bill had done in a similar situation) that a "close friend" had died, he was not permitted to take a leave of absence because the administration could not understand how the death of a close friend would necessitate such a leave.

Friends planned a "tribute celebration" for Allyn after his body was taken back to Wisconsin by his family. Yellow daffodils were given to all Allyn's friends who gathered in Boston's Arlington Street Church. Friends presented poems, talked about Allyn's life, played music. Allyn's community marked his death with feelings of sadness and springtime.

Drug abuse can play a similar role to alcohol abuse in the suicides of gay men and lesbians. In 1980, the *San Francisco Chronicle* reported the suicide of a 29 year old gay man who was "Distraught over the imminent loss of his temporary job and the end of an affair with a male lover." Thomas McGuire jumped from the 14th floor of a San Francisco office building to his death after leaving a three-page handwritten letter addressed to the press. In the letter, McGuire wrote:

> As a matter of fact my drug usage has only been for the last three years and already I have lost three jobs because of it and even more important to me—a possible long-lasting love relationship . . . A lasting love relationship has been something I have yearned for the last 10 years of my life and it has never come about . . . Please print this . . . in the daily newspaper or *Advocate* as the last request of a dying man and for the betterment of mankind so that the many others who have my problem may not resort to the same violent ordeal I am about to endure. I am twenty-nine and every [sic] since I was nineteen or when I first went into the military, I have been gay or homosexual as you wish and my life has been governed more or less by one predominant factor—an oversexual drive. Now there is essentially nothing wrong with one being oversexed but there is when one becomes dominated by that drive and especially when one lets drug involvement intervene the way I did . . . I was hoping that I might meet my dreamboy through drugs. I really enjoyed the feelings created by the drugs and sexual intercourse was the best I ever had . . .[17]

What is needed these days to prevent others from continuing in patterns of depression, alcohol and drug abuse, and suicide attempts is the development of programs specifically geared for the alcoholic and drug-abusing gay man or lesbian. Such programs have been launched through clinics providing medical and mental health care to this population, through special Alcoholics Anonymous programs, and through the development of small counseling groups for alcohol or drug dependent gay people.[18] Programs that do not cater specifically to gay people are probably still dealing with a large percentage of the lesbian and gay male substance-abusing population and they must educate themselves on the special needs of this population. By ignoring the special problems that a lesbian alcoholic, for example, presents, programs will be doing a service to no one. Their treatment of the individual will be less than adequate and may tend to intensify the woman's feelings of isolation and "difference." Only by bringing the issue into the open and addressing the woman's lesbianism as an aspect of her life which she needs to feel positively about, will the program be truly effective. Alcoholism is one way lesbians and gay men deal with our anger and pain at societal attitudes. This fact must be recognized in dealing with gay clients.

The lesbian and gay community must also address the issue of alcoholism as it looks at the role suicide plays in our community. Alcohol-free spaces have been developed by many women's communities in recognition of the problems many lesbians and other women have with alcohol. The gay male community must address the problem in a similar way. While so many gay men's lives will continue to revolve around bars, discos and parties where alcohol freely flows and is, in fact, often pushed on people by bar personnel, the creation of alternative socializing spaces will bring about an easier life for gay male alcoholics. Until we recognize substance abuse as a problem, rather than accept it as a part of gay masculinity as it is of straight masculinity, gay men will continue to fight an uphill battle against alcohol abuse.

6.

Areas for Continued Research

Thus far, this book has looked at individual lesbians and gay men whose suicides or suicide attempts involve factors which pertain to lesbians and gay men in ways distinct from the population at large: substance abuse, blackmail and exposure, youth, holiday periods and the "coming out" process. While these factors may not be entirely unique to the gay community, they function very specifically among lesbians and gay men to increase chances of suicide amid an already high risk population. For example, alcoholism increases any person's risk for suicide, but unless counselors working with a lesbian alcoholic understand the important role alcohol plays in much of the lesbian community, they will not be able to effectively help this woman. Holidays are difficult times for many people and may be especially depressing periods for large numbers of gay men who, because they have acknowledged their homosexuality to their parents, are cut off from their families. Developing an understanding and ability to help suicidal lesbians and gay men requires an understanding both of the needs of depressed and suicidal people in general and the special needs of depressed and suicidal lesbians and gay men.

There are many areas where substantial research and study still need to be done. It is ironic that book after book has been researched and written examining *why* people are gay and whether lesbianism and male homosexuality are "morally acceptable," yet so little has been written to help lesbians and gay men lead happier and healthier lives. We need much more information on many aspects of gay suicide: elderly lesbians and gay men who kill themselves, specific sexual practices in relationship to suicide and suicide fantasies, and the experiences transvestites and transsexuals have had with suicide. Because of the total lack of information on these topics, I can only urge researchers to consider their importance in future studies.

Other areas which lack substantial information include the suicides of closeted homosexuals, the role of suicide among lesbians and gay men of color, and the ways in which gay people who have experienced the loss of a lover become susceptible to thoughts of suicide. The sparse information available has been synthesized in this chapter to provide a cursory look at these issues. Women and men who have never acknowledged their homosexuality—sexually or politically—are clearly a hidden population that needs to be studied carefully in this regard. These people are perhaps the most difficult population to reach and help because so much of their pain and conflict is repressed and disguised. Many lesbians and gay men of color have traditionally been encouraged to feel that suicide is a "white issue," and thus the suicides of Native Americans, Hispanics, blacks and Asians have been without documentation or analysis. Recent research indicates, however, that suicide exists in these populations in a manner distinct from white people, and professionals helping a Chicana lesbian cannot assume that risk factors and treatment needs for her are identical with those of white lesbians or white women. Unfortunately, virtually no information is available on suicide among Hispanic,[1] Asian and Native American lesbians and gay men and very little work has focused on black lesbians and gay men. More of a priority must be given to understanding the health needs of these populations. The final topic in this chapter involves the loss of a lover. Substantial research has been done among heterosexual widows and widowers or divorced and separated people on this topic, but very little on lesbians and gay men. I hope to draw attention to these areas that need additional study and research.

CLOSETED HOMOSEXUALS

One factor that makes it extremely difficult to obtain accurate suicide statistics for lesbians and gay men is the inability of many women and men with homosexual feelings to identify or act on these feelings. The stigma of identifying oneself as gay, or functioning as a lesbian or gay man in our culture, forces many people to avoid any erotic contact with others of the same sex. And, as we know, feelings of alienation and depression are rife among sexually repressed people. Studies indicate that a satisfying sex life is a deterrent to suicidal feelings.[2] When repressed sexuality *is* a factor in a person's suicide, it is difficult to document.

Marshall Bloom's suicide is such a death.[3] Bloom was a leading figure in the antiwar movement of the 1960s. While still a student at Amherst College, he served as editor of the campus newspaper and introduced a radical political perspective. He has been credited with instigating a walkout at Amherst's 1966 commencement activities protesting the presence of then Secretary of Defense Robert McNamara and organizing student uprisings while at the London School of Economics. He was instrumental in the founding of Liberation News Service in 1967 and in splitting off from LNS in 1968 and organizing another radical news service. Bloom has become a folk hero of the late 60s, featured in several books by Ray Mungo and Steve Diamond.[4]

Friends and colleagues maintain that Bloom was also homosexual. Allen Young, in a tribute to Bloom in *Fag Rag*, wrote, "Marshall Bloom was a faggot, and his faggotry was part of his life, as it was part of his death."[5] Another friend wrote that Bloom "believed he was a homosexual."[6] While we may never know whether or not Bloom was ever overtly sexually involved with other men, it is clear from those who knew him that Bloom's life and death involved coming to terms with his feelings for other men and with being a "faggoty" man.

Bloom was tall, thin and unusually demonstrative with his voice and gestures. He often waved and fluttered his hands as he spoke in a way that is not a traditionally acceptable manner for men. His demonstrativeness was noticed by other people, and friends and co-workers talked behind his back, speculating on his "effeminacy." Allen Young wrote, "The truth is that Marshall had GAY written all over him, especially when he talked and moved."[7]

In the summer of 1967 he was fired from his position as the director of the Collegiate Press Service, an alliance of student newspapers. While some sources attributed his dismissal to his radical politics or his use of drugs, in the dismissal proceedings his effeminacy was discussed and was a prime factor in some negative attitudes towards him which led to his removal.

Bloom appears to have discussed ambivalent feelings and sexual confusion with several close friends, although many believe that he never acted on his attraction to other men. He had intense sexual feelings for some of the activist men he worked with, yet he repressed them. One of these men was killed in an automobile crash, and Bloom wrote an article in LNS which conveyed his powerful feelings in a guarded manner.

On November 1, 1969, All Soul's Day, Bloom ran a vacuum cleaner hose from the exhaust of his green Triumph through the car window and died of asphyxiation. His death was treated "as though it were some kind of ultimate yippie stunt" by his straight movement friends, and Bloom was portrayed as "a mysterious magical figure, a shaman."[8] It is too easy to see Bloom's suicide as a stunt or a political action. This ignores the important role of self-image and personal feelings in a suicide; it depersonalizes and distorts suicide. Likewise, David Eisenhower, several years later, dragged up Bloom's suicide on the op-ed page of the *New York Times*, blaming the factionalism of the movement and the "disillusionment" and "alienation" of radicals for his death.[9] Eisenhower used Bloom as a symbol of the demise of the left and of the left's inability to provide an alternative to the traditional American system. Again, the man's suicide is depersonalized, analyzed at a distance, and his sexuality and human qualities are ignored.

One cannot hope to provide a complete explanation for a person's suicide—the reasons are intensely personal and often go unstated. But two people who knew Bloom acknowledge that his confusion over his sexuality must have played a part. Judith Coburn, in a letter to the *Times* in response to Eisenhower's piece, attributed the suicide to Bloom's failure to "manage an accommodation with the values and lifestyle of the society in which he was born" and his homosexual feelings: "He believed he was a homosexual. Others have written eloquently of the repression and self-doubt that our society visits on those who do not conform sexually. Perhaps the Gay Liberation Movement might have helped, I don't know."[10]

Allen Young also sees the role that Bloom's ambivalent feelings about his sexuality must have played in his suicide; he wrote, "It is not enough to say that Marshall was a lonely, unfulfilled person. Marshall was a lonely, unfulfilled *faggot*."[11] Bloom's suicide took place shortly after he had tried to initiate a romantic and sexual relationship with a woman friend, an attempt that did not succeed. His inability to express his sexual feelings toward men certainly must have had a powerful effect on his self-image.

The suicides of homosexual men and women who have never acknowledged their homosexuality to another person or engaged in sexual activity with a person of their same sex are difficult to analyze. Dr. Robert Litman has stated that there are suicides of middle-aged businessmen which apparently have homosexual origins but are not very often identified as such.[12] Another psychiatrist has written:

> The suicidal person who expresses fears of impotence, imaginary venereal disease or unworthiness as a sexual partner may be putting up a smokescreen for himself and others for an inner resistance to heterosexuality. So long as external sources may be

blamed, the underlying homosexual fears may go unnoticed. The single person who "has to support his mother" or who "always finds an impossible marital partner" may be defending against an underlying sexual confusion which makes heterosexuality impossible. In a society where status accompanies sexual potency, great anxiety may accompany failure to form a satisfactory heterosexual relationship.[13]

Thus the discussion and debate concerning who was and who was not a homosexual extends even into the realm of suicides. Should this book include a look at the suicides of Virginia Woolf, Sylvia Plath or Ernest Hemingway, because some people consider them repressed homosexuals or bisexuals? While I have specifically decided not to include such people here, those who are deeply closeted and never acknowledge homosexual feelings are a potential source of future research for suicidologists and lesbian and gay health workers.

BLACK SUICIDE

Little attention has been given to suicide among black people, either by the black community or by psychiatrists and suicidologists studying suicidal people. Because studies have indicated that white people kill themselves two to three times as frequently as other racial groups it has been easy to ignore the very real problem of suicide among black people and focus on suicide as a "white problem." This pattern of reasoning is also used by many heterosexual black people when considering lesbianism and male homosexuality. In a dialogue published in *This Bridge Called My Back: Writings by Radical Women of Color*, Barbara Smith and Beverly Smith discussed the tendency of the black community to avoid some difficult issues in this way:

Beverly: This country is so racist that it is possible to take many, many things and concepts that have nothing to do with race and talk about them in racial terms. Because people are so dichotomized into either black or white, it defines a continuum. This is so strict and so overwhelming in this country, you can take things that have nothing to do with race and refer to them racially.

Therefore, Black people have the option of taking things— sexuality behavior, conflicts, whatever they don't like—and saying, "That's white." Lesbianism is not the only thing seen as a white thing. A real good example is suicide. Black people say, "Yeah, suicide is a white thing."

Barbara: Oh yeah, we used to believe that. And of course one felt all the worse for having considered it. I'm thinking of Ntozake

Shange's play "for colored girls who have considered suicide." It's very brave. I mean she's dealing with a lot of myths, by saying that we have even considered it, if it's supposed to be a white thing.[14]

Because of the prevalence of these myths among researchers we have very little information available on suicidal black lesbians and gay men. People researching and studying suicide have allowed the racial breakdown of statistics to serve as an excuse for their failure to address the suicides of blacks. Statistics cannot legitimize racism, especially when recent research on suicide among black people indicates that suicide *is* an issue for the black community.[15]

While some researchers have attempted to deny the validity of the studies which indicate that the rate of black suicide is lower than that of white suicide, others who have given close scrutiny to existing studies have arrived at some startling conclusions. Suicide among young black people has tremendously increased over the past two decades—as has the suicide rate for youth in general—so that currently the suicide rate of black men between the ages of 20–24 approximates and at times surpasses the rate for white men of the same ages.[16] One suicidologist wrote, "Among young black urban adults between the ages of 20 to 35, suicide has been considerably higher than among their white counterparts."[17] Another study has indicated that the suicide rate for women of color between the ages of 15–19 is greater than the rate for white women of the same age.[18] Perhaps what is most striking is that statistics indicate that blacks between the ages of 15–24 commit suicide at a rate higher than that of the total black population of all ages.[19] This indicates a very basic distinction between the suicides of black people and white people in America: while the suicide rate for white people increases with age, for black people the rate generally tends to decline with increasing age.

The only statistics available on black lesbians and gay men and suicide indicate that they tend to attempt suicide or seriously consider suicide at a rate less than white homosexuals, yet greater than heterosexual blacks. Of the black lesbians interviewed for the Bell & Weinberg study, 25% indicated that they had seriously considered or attempted suicide, as compared to 41% of the white lesbians and 19% of the black heterosexual women. Twenty-four percent of the black gay men had seriously considered or attempted suicide, compared to 37% of the white homosexual men and only 2% of the black heterosexual men.[20] While these statistics are not based on a substantial sampling of the black population, they do indicate that approximately a quarter of the black lesbian and gay male population has had suicide as a serious issue in their lives at some point.

Understanding these statistics is difficult. One psychotherapist wrote:

> Despite her isolation, the Black lesbian is less likely to contemplate suicide than her white counterpart. The Black lesbian's attitude is one of survival. A friend of mine calls this the "make do" syndrome, while I refer to it as "there's no such thing as can't." Historically, Black women have experienced some of the most brutal and adverse conditions imaginable, and they have survived. This survival resulted from a knowledge passed on through Black culture, which taught them an ethos of "you must." One need only read the words of Toni Morrison, Zora Neale Hurston, Alice Walker and Angela Davis to understand the characteristic survival of black women.[21]

Other researchers have written:

> Blacks as a minority have been exploited and discriminated against for centuries and appear to have developed a consciousness of self-preservation in the white society. As Gibbs and Martin demonstrated, blacks in the United States have greater status integration than whites, and are for this reason less likely to kill themselves.[22]

Apparently substantial efforts have been made to understand why it appears that fewer blacks than whites commit suicide, while little energy has been put into understanding the special problems of the black population as pertains to suicide.

Herbert Hendin has done considerable research and work on black suicide, which begins to probe important issues such as the connection between suicide, homicide and violence among young black people.[23] Hendin's interviews with suicidal black people indicate that often the black person who has attempted suicide is as likely to attempt murder. Hendin wrote:

> Many of the patients came alive only through acts or fantasies of violence. Merely talking of past fights or brutality made them far more animated than usual. Often they saw living itself as an act of violence and death as the only way to control their rage. Perhaps this explains the long periods of emotional death that punctuated their violent acts or the variety of deaths-in-life that they used to keep their anger in check.[24]

Unfortunately, Hendin's research on black gay men and suicide tends to be marred by a pervasive homophobia which leads him to conclusions that appear to be based more on prejudice than on fact.

Hendin asserts that: "The relation of race to self-hatred and violence was particularly apparent in the suicidal black men who were also homosexuals."[25] He goes on to say that these black men "generally ... preferred white partners" (Hendin adds that this "also proved true of nonsuicidal black homosexuals") and, for them, "the homosexual act included a symbolic incorporation of whiteness ... and could, if only temporarily relieve them of the pervasive feeling of being loathsome 'black bugs.'" Hendin's conclusion that, for some gay black men, "a white partner served to intensify their sense of being dirty or degraded" appears too simplistic and unsupported by adequate information and documentation.

Hendin also found that black male homosexuals often tended to have violent fathers and, in later life, directed their anger at both their fathers and their mothers. This appears to him to be distinct from black heterosexuals who tend to select their mothers as the target for their anger. Hendin concludes that the violence of their fathers is the root cause of both a black man's homosexuality *and* his tendency towards suicide. Black lesbians appear to have been ignored in his research.

Hendin's writing provides a prime example of the difficulty in finding reliable information and statistics on black lesbians and gay men and suicide. Articles like his which focus on black suicide tend to ignore lesbians and gay men or else treat the stereotypes and the myths rather than real lives.

Hendin's analysis of the reasons why black youth may be more susceptible to suicide than white youth is interesting and certainly pertinent to black lesbians and gay men during their teens and twenties:

> It does not seem surprising that suicide becomes a problem at such a relatively early age for the black person. A sense of despair, a feeling that life will never be satisfying, confronts many blacks at a far younger age than it does most whites. For most discontented white people the young adult years contain the hope of a change for the better. The marked rise in white suicide after 45 reflects, among other things, the waning of such hope that is bound to accompany age. The blacks who survive the dangerous years between 20 and 35 have made some accommodation with life—a compromise that has usually included a scaling down of their aspirations.[26]

Hendin's belief that the twenties and thirties are a time when blacks either face reality and cope with the difficulties that confront them in life or else turn towards violence as a means of grappling with their world may seem simplistic, but, until further research is done on black people and suicide, it will remain one of the few theories available to us in medical literature.

While the suicides and suicide attempts of black lesbians and gay men may appear to offer information on the ways in which individual black women and men cope with racism and gay oppression, many of the suicides appear to have little to do with racial matters.

In a biography of Bessie Smith, the black blues singer, Chris Albertson writes candidly about Smith's relationships with women.[27] One of her long-term lovers, Lillian Simpson, was a member of Bessie's musical troupe and the two women toured the country together performing their show. Albertson reports that, one day, Bessie walked up behind Lillian and kissed her in front of another person. Lillian reacted with embarrassment and pulled away from Bessie, telling her, "Don't play around with me like that." Bessie reacted with fury, the two women exchanged heated words and for three days and nights Bessie did not acknowledge Lillian's presence.

The following evening Lillian did not arrive at the theatre and the troupe performed without her. Bessie became concerned after the show and then another woman ran in and said, "I passed Lillian's room, I saw an envelope sticking out from under the door. The door was locked, so I pulled the envelope out, opened it and saw that it was a suicide note. That's when I ran back to the theatre to get Bessie."

Bessie and others immediately dashed to the hotel next door. They smelled gas coming from Lillian's room, attempted to break through the door, and then Bessie ran for the hotel manager who opened it. Bessie found Lillian lying on the bed unconscious. She had nailed the window closed so they broke open the pane. An ambulance took Lillian to a hospital.

Bessie arrived at the hospital the following day to take Lillian out. "From that day on," a friend said, "she [Lillian] didn't care where or when Bessie kissed her—she got real bold."

While Lillian's suicide attempt may seem to be right out of the pages of a gothic novel, such attempts are not uncommon when a lover—homosexual or heterosexual—has been spurned.

Many deaths of black people which are actually homicides are certified by police and medical authorities as accidents or suicides. The black community is vulnerable to this abuse of suicides of black people as a political weapon to show the "instability," "violence" and "decadence" of their community. Black people are also victimized by police and government officials who conceal murder by calling it "suicide."

During the early days of gay liberation in New York City, Raymond Lavon Moore, a black gay man who was held in the New York City prison, the Tombs, was murdered by "the authorities." His death was reported as a suicide and the Gay Community Prisoner Defense Committee was formed as a response to the deception. The Young Lords conducted an investigation of their own into Moore's death and concluded that he was, in fact, murdered by prison guards. Another man who was also held on the fourth floor of the Tombs, Richard Harris, issued a public statement declaring that Moore had been beaten to death.[28]

Much more specific information is needed before work to prevent the suicides of black lesbians and gay men will be effective. Studies of this population must look carefully at the different factors that pertain to feelings of self-destructiveness and must integrate in it an analysis of the varying roles of racism, sexism, classism and homophobia.

THE LOSS OF A LOVER

The loss of a lover, either through death or "divorce," is a difficult experience for people of any sexual orientation. The emotional distress and pain of breaking off a relationship can be so overwhelming as to deeply affect even the most stable person. Losing a lover through death can leave one feeling angry, empty, lonely, and without clear focus for one's feelings. Periods of such great loss leave one vulnerable to strong depressions and desires to commit suicide.

The situation is compounded for lesbians and gay men. Sally Casper, codirector of the Samaritans, a suicide prevention service in Boston, said, "For a gay person who has lost his or her partner, if the person isn't out of the closet, there's no sympathy from co-workers or friends or family. A loss that's socially not recognized cuts the person off from the normal channels for mourning and getting over it. Loss of a lover is a normal problem that can happen to everyone; but it might be worse for gay people."[29]

This book has already provided examples of how gay people were denied the normal mechanisms for grieving because of societal denial of same-sex primary relationships. Allyn's lover was denied leave from his teaching job, and Bill had a similar experience, because administrators did not award such leaves at the deaths of "close friends." Having to hide or deny one's grief because one can't fully disclose information on the nature of one's relationships can intensify feelings of sorrow and alienation.

The suicide of Francis Otto Matthiessen, Harvard professor, literary critic and political activist, involved many factors but, while the suicide occurred in 1950, it is only recently that Matthiessen's sorrow and loneliness at the death of his lifelong lover Russell Cheney has been recognized as a factor. While people have preferred to see Matthiessen's suicide in terms of his involvement in progressive politics during an era of increasing repression, it is apparent that Matthiessen's feelings about his homosexuality and his relationship with Cheney were significant factors contributing to his death.

The twenty-year relationship between these two men, which lasted from their meeting on a sea voyage in 1924 to Cheney's death in 1945, can only be described as a loving union of two remarkable individuals.[30] What is most exciting about the relationship is that we are fortunate to have documentation of the intimate communication between them which has survived in their almost daily correspondence throughout the twenty years. Since both men traveled extensively and spent large portions of each year apart, their letters remain primary source material for understanding the men both as individuals and as a couple. Through the letters, we are able to chart Matthiessen's periods of depression and anxiety as well as his ambivalent attitude towards his homosexuality.[31] In addition to his reactions to attractive men he sees on the street, his attitude towards masturbation ("self-abuse"), and his musings regarding the origins of his homosexuality, the letters reveal an attitude and a philosophy based on the work of early sexologists that contains pride and understanding closely akin to gay liberationist attitudes. As Matthiessen and Cheney correspond about the best way to inform their friends of the nature of their relationship, the role of monogamy in romance, and Matthiessen's insecurity about a possible strain of effeminacy in his lecture voice ("Am I just like any fairy?"), we come to realize that the issues gay men and lesbians struggle with today, as individuals and in their relationships, are issues which some same-sex couples have explored for years. For the uninformed reader, these letters dispel the myth many of us maintain that gay identity was unknown before 1969.

Matthiessen and Cheney met on the ship *Paris* during September, 1924, when Matthiessen was on his way to Oxford as a graduate student and Cheney was resuming his travels in Europe. At the time, Cheney was 43 years old and Matthiessen was 23. Cheney's family wealth allowed him to pursue his career as an artist, and Matthiessen, whose family had little money, had been granted a fellowship at Oxford. As Matthiessen said in a letter to a friend, "We fell into an easy intimacy from the start." Matthiessen soon realized that, "in order to be on a basis of complete truth and freedom with him I must drag out the skeleton of my twisted psychology that I had [disclosed to a few intimate friends in New Haven several months before]."

As gay men today experience much apprehension before sharing information such as this with friends, so Matthiessen spent the day before he told Cheney (who later came to call himself "Rat") about himself, summoning up all his courage and strength. Matthiessen writes,

> Came two o'clock, and we went down to our cabins. Now, I said, steeled by desperation, now, now, I'll never get up courage enough if I don't do it now. So I sat Rat down in a chair in my cabin on the pretense of giving him some fruit before we went to bed. And while his mouth was stuffed with a pear, I said in a voice that attempted to maintain its usual pass the bread, please conversational tone, but which sounded queer and remote for all that:
> "I know it won't make any difference to our friendship, but there's one thing I've got to tell you: before [my extraordinary senior year at Yale] I was sexually inverted. Of course I've controlled it since . . ."
> The munching of the pear died away. There followed perhaps half a minute of the most heavily freighted silence I have ever felt. Then, in a far away voice I had never heard came the answer: "My God, feller, you've turned me upside down. I'm that way too."[32]

Matthiessen's attitude towards his homosexuality at the time was based on theories of sexual inversion developed twenty years earlier. He had read Havelock Ellis during the preceding spring and it is clear that much of his conception of his own homosexuality came from Ellis' work. Matthiessen seems to have had two contradictory strains within him regarding his sexuality. On one hand, he seems to refer to sex with men as "sordid" and "depressing." Matthiessen was attracted but, simultaneously, repulsed by such experiences. A man he notices at the Marble Arch at Hyde Park ("The place in London most flagrant") attracts him, yet he describes the man as "luscious slime." He finds inspiration, however, in Whitman's poetry for his love of men and has a realistic, though strong, attitude about societal reaction to homosexual men:

> Can't you hear the hell-hounds of society baying full pursuit behind us? But that's just the point. We are beyond society. We've said thank you very much, and stepped outside and closed the door. In the eyes of the unknowing world we are a talented artist of wealth and position and a promising young graduate student.

In the eyes of the knowing world we would be pariahs, outlaws, degenerates. This is indeed the price we pay for the unforgivable sin of being born different from the great run of mankind.[33]

On reading Edward Carpenter's *The Imtermediate Sex,* Matthiessen is excited by "the idea that what we have is one of the divine gifts," checks off specific passages and sends Cheney the copy.

During the first year of their relationship, Matthiessen became increasingly comfortable with his feelings about himself and Cheney and moved towards discussing their relationship with some close friends. Cheney panicked and wrote to Matthiessen that perhaps they should end the sexual aspect of their friendship and be "two regular fellers." Clearly Cheney was experiencing the conflict many gay men feel at different times in their lives; he wrote, "Now I imagine you are saying I am a hell of a feller to act under the pressure of opinion in this way . . .Well I have sneaked drinks long enough. I have sneaked into parks and toilets long enough, and I will do neither of them any more."

Matthiessen answered his friend patiently and with reason and honesty, He matched Cheney's argument point for point, saying:

That to me is the essence of it: we were born as we are. I am no longer the least ashamed of it. What is there to be ashamed of? It simply reveals the fact that sex is not mathematical and clear-cut, something to be separated definitely into male and female; but that just as there are energetic, active women and sensitive delicate men, so also there are women who appear to be feminine but have a male sex element, and men, like us, who appear to be masculine but have a female sex element. Ashamed of it? Forty years ago, perhaps, when nothing was really known about it, I would have felt myself an outcast. But now that the matter has been studied scientifically, and the facts are there in black and white? No, accept it, just the way you accept the fact that you have two legs.[34]

Gradually, Cheney relaxed from his frightened position and the men overcame the crisis in their relationship.

It appears that Matthiessen's conflicting feelings about his homosexuality were never resolved. By entering into the relationship with Cheney, Matthiessen was able to feel comfortable about his homosexuality. On a trip to England, Matthiessen describes his reaction to a man that belies his self-conscious attempt to assume Whitman's sexual enthusiasm for the working man:

Going into the cathedral this morning we passed a workman— husky, broad-shouldered, 40, the perfect Chaucerian yeoman. He caught my eye—both as a magnificently built feller, and as fitting in so perfectly to the type of fourteenth century workman. He might just as well have been building the original cathedral, as repairing it centuries later.

Afterwards while I was standing alone in the choir he came up and said: "Fine old building, sir." His voice was unusually gentle, his eye a dark full brown. We stood there talking about a quarter of a minute, and as he went on I deliberately let my elbow rub against his belly. That was all: there couldn't have been anything more. I didn't want anything more. I was simply attracted by him as a simple open-hearted feller, and wanted to feel the touch of his body as a passing gesture. I had a hard on, but there was no question of not wanting to keep myself for you. For a passing gesture is one thing, but you can give the deepest spring of your life *with its full significance*—the passionate uncontrolled offering of your body—only to the man you love.[35]

It appears that Matthiessen retained an attitude that continued to view sexual activity with men as somehow tainted and dirty. His relationship with Cheney was absolved from this and thus he retreated into it. As he writes to Cheney, "These other friends of ours have wives, Pictor, and in their love for them lies their refuge and serenity. But we have been alone, and here is our God-given chance not to be alone. I need you, Pictor, now and for the rest of my life." When Matthiessen confronts the "falseness of my position in the world" ("Have I any right in a community that would so utterly disapprove of me if it knew the facts?"), his comforting response to Cheney is, "I need you, feller; for together we can confront whatever there is."

Throughout the letters to Cheney, Matthiessen occasionally makes disparaging remarks about other homosexual men. The *Dictionary of American Biography,* however reliable that might be in its attitudes towards homosexuality, also states that "he was unusually hostile to homosexual colleagues who mixed their academic and sexual relations" and that "his circle was more predominantly heterosexual than was usual in Harvard literary groups of the time."[36] While his relationship with Cheney allowed him to find an identity with which he could comfortably live his life, it is clear that Matthiessen was not at peace with his homosexuality.

Matthiessen's struggle with suicidal feelings and depression began about five years after meeting Cheney. At the end of a New Year's day letter to Cheney, Matthiessen writes, "How I want to live! You'll help me, won't you, dear feller." Over the next decade Matthiessen was overwhelmed at times by depressions that were exacerbated by a heavy work schedule at Harvard, his work on his masterpiece *American Renaissance*, and Cheney's ill health and bouts with alcoholism. During one lapse, Cheney shocked Matthiessen by insisting that he wanted to die. This began to develop in Matthiessen the fear that Cheney might die and leave him alone.

In December, 1938, Matthiessen became troubled by insomnia and, as a friend wrote, "there was no doubt that his clear critical mind . . .was now in disarray being turned inward upon himself." Friends persuaded Matthiessen to commit himself to McLean Hospital, a sanatorium outside Boston, where he remained for 19 days. A letter to Cheney three days after he was admitted reflects his spirit during a very troubled time: "I am fighting this obscure demon, and all I ask of you is to try not to worry, to give your anxiety over to the doctors, and to keep your own warm balance. And if things get tough for you nervously, don't hesitate to call on Fleming, but mostly, feller, *live*, hold onto this rare thing we have, and that will help me find my way back to the light."[37]

Matthiessen began to keep a journal during his stay at McLean Hospital and in it he confronts his deep fears that Cheney might die and leave him to confront life alone. He recalls a night where he fantasized about jumping out of windows and at first told himself that it is his work that has created the tension. When his doctor told him "No one kills himself over a book," he was forced to probe more deeply. Matthiessen wrote,

> Towards the end of my session with Dr. Fremont-Smith he dwelt on the danger of fear, and perhaps intuitively introduced the fear of the death of someone you loved. At once I raised the question of whether I could face life without Russell, and saw again the fear that gripped me so fiercely at that moment in the fall, in September when he had gone home after the hurricane, and had gotten caught by drink, as I knew he would, and had finally called from the Copley and I had gone down and brought him back, and lying on the bed the next morning his hands still shaking desperately from the nervous shock, he had said that he had wanted to die. That moment stunned me. It brought out what has probably been latent for a long time. I have not been given at all to worry or to fear, and now I am tangled in them. Having built my life so simply and wholly with Russell's, having had my eyes opened by him to so much beauty, my heart filled by such richness, my pulse beating steadily in time with his in intimate daily companionship, I am shocked at the thought of life without him. How would it be possible? How go on from day to day?[38]

As much as Matthiessen preferred to see his fear of Cheney's death as the "nub of the problem," it is clear that deeper issues plagued him. "Much of the iceberg lies hidden. Barrett talks of the aggression that I am now turning against myself, and God knows I have been knifing my confidence, rubbing salt into the wounds of my self-esteem." Yet Matthiessen seems never to have been able to grasp these issues.

Over the next seven years, Matthiessen seemed to have attained a more balanced mental state. He became involved in progressive politics and helped to begin the Harvard Teachers Union and was a board member of the Massachusetts Civil Liberties Union. Matthiessen's book *American Renaissance*[39] was published to tremendous critical praise and he was made an Associate Professor at Harvard. The attack on Pearl Harbor had a considerable effect on the university administration, which continued to shift emphasis away from the humanities and onto sciences and the development of weaponry.

Cheney's health was not good and his frequent illnesses—tuberculosis, pneumonia, alcoholism—kept him apart from Matthiessen much of the time. Winters were spent in the warmer Southwest and much of spring and summer was spent in and out of sanatoriums. This put tremendous strain on Matthiessen, who was working hard at maintaining his own mental balance in the midst of increased demands on him by Harvard, his writing, and the political climate.

Cheney returned to their home in Maine for the summer of 1945 but his health was not good. On July 12, he suffered an attack of asthma and "was knocked unconscious during the night by a thrombosis." Cheney died the next day at the age of 63.

Matthiessen had to face a very difficult family funeral in Connecticut. Cheney's niece Helen Knapp, a friend of Matthiessen's, traveled with him to the funeral and later wrote:

> I think he was partly aware of the emotional conflicts and frustrations in store for him in that complicated maze of antagonistic human relations. I was only dimly aware in advance, not only of my own torn-apart strands of conflicting loyalties in the part I'd be called upon to play, but my own agonized pity for Matty, my indignation at such a situation, and, in addition, my terrible sense of loss of the uncle I loved so much. I rather guessed Matty did not fully sense the hostile atmosphere he was to contend with in Russell's family, which he must bear in addition to his already fearful load of loneliness and sorrow . . .[40]

In her recounting of the family funeral it is clear that no public acknowledgment was made of Matthiessen's relationship with Cheney, and Knapp writes that "Currents of ill feeling passed from the Cheney family to the man they knew in their hearts had more of Russell's heart and mind than they had."

Matthiessen had to face life alone, without Cheney, and it was a difficult world he entered. The United States dropped the bomb on Hiroshima and Nagasaki within a month of Cheney's funeral. Life at Harvard was increasingly succumbing to the repression of the times. Over the final five years of his life several old friends died and Matthiessen felt increasingly alienated from progressive politics. He continued to write prolifically and teach his classes, but even there his personal feelings of pain and loss came through in his lectures. Kenneth Lynn, professor and critic and a former student of Matthiessen, wrote about his teacher's work at this time,

> Like many of his favorite American writers, Matthiessen was haunted by the feelings of loss and anguish they expressed. An almost unbearable undercurrent of personal suffering ran through his lectures at times. For example, in an analysis I heard him give of "Mr. Flood's Party" in the summer of 1946, he incorporated his own desolation within E. A. Robinson's, as he had good reason to do. Matthiessen and his most intimate friend, the painter Russell Cheney, had owned a house together in Kittery, Maine, an hour's drive or so from the Tilbury Town of Robinson's poetry. Cheney, however, had died in 1945, and in the summer of 1946, Matthiessen was trying to get used to living at Kittery without him. Listening to the sadness in Matthiessen's voice as he worked his way through the poem, I was sure that Eben Flood was not the only man who ever stood on a hilltop in the state of Maine, talking to himself, with only whiskey for company . . .[41]

Matthiessen's reaction to Cheney's death was to fully throw himself into his work. He became so involved in conferences, political groups, writing and teaching that, as one friend wrote, he "looked like a man hurrying across a pond of ice cakes, jumping from one cake to another as the last one sank."[42] Almost five years hurried past him, leaving him depressed, exhausted and saddened.

On March 31, 1950, Matthiessen checked into a room at Boston's Manger Hotel. After a last dinner with friends, he went to his apartment and left notes and arranged his papers for his friends. He went back to the hotel and ended his life by leaping from the window of his twelfth-floor room.

The newspapers the following day, as well as subsequent writings on Matthiessen, have tended to view his suicide primarily as an act of political frustration. Matthiessen's suicide note seems to encourage this interpretation:

> I have taken this room in order to do what I have to do. My will is to be found on my desk in my apartment at 87 Pinckney Street, Boston. Here are the keys—Please notify Harvard University— where I have been a professor.
>
> I am exhausted. I have been subject to so many severe depressions during the past few years that I can no longer believe that I can continue to be of use to my profession and my friends. I hope that my friends will be able to believe that I still love them in spite of this desperate act.
>
> Francis Otto Matthiessen
>
> How much the state of the world has to do with the state of my mind I do not know. But as a Christian and as a Socialist believing in international peace, I find myself terribly oppressed by the present tensions.[43]

Obituaries and explanations of Matthiessen's suicide have tended to trivialize or ignore his difficulty in getting beyond his grief at Cheney's death. The *Boston Sunday Globe* (April 2, 1950) ran the story under the headline, "Harvard Man Called Casualty of Cold War," and stated that Matthiessen "leaped to his death because of depression over world conditions." Oliver Allen of the Massachusetts Progressive Party is credited with describing Matthiessen as "a casualty of the cold war" and charged further that Matthiessen was "hounded and persecuted by evil men" and finally "broke under the strain."

The New York Times (April 2, 1950) explained that "exhaustion brought on by literary research and depression inspired by world conditions were blamed by associates today for the fatal leap of Professor Francis Otto Matthiessen of Harvard, authority on American literature and a self-styled Socialist." The *Times* quoted Howard Fast, of the writing and publishing division of the New York State Council of the Arts, Sciences and Professions, as saying "Professor Matthiessen is as surely a victim of the cold war and the Truman-Acheson foreign policy as those who face blacklists, jail and academic witch hunts. He, however, paid with his life."

Perhaps most offensive in the attempts of the press to turn Matthiessen's tragic suicide into political martyrdom was the *Boston Herald* (April 3, 1950) editorial "Tales of a Suicide" in which the paper attempted to explain the suicide as the act of a man whose political dream had gone sour:

> It is unlikely that Professor Matthiessen chose death because his fight for the left had become arduous. It is unlikely, despite his last testament, that the poor prospect for peace disturbed him. It is likely that somehow he began to doubt the validity of the things he had held essential, that maybe the good life could not be simply arranged by having a powerful government spread its bounty among the poor . . .
>
> The moral might be that America need have no fear while it holds firm in its faith, the faith that good comes from good works and not from evil means, that a society is for the individual in it, not for some vision that must be bought by repression and cruelty. We have something worth fighting for, something worth living for.

Matthiessen's friends and colleagues were concerned with these attempts to turn his suicide into a political statement and even more concerned at the attempts to portray him as a communist or a communist sympathizer. The *Globe* (April 2, 1950) article stated that Matthiessen was "often accused of Communist sympathies" and that, in his suicide note, he described himself as a "Christian and a Socialist." *The New York Times* (April 2, 1950) mentioned Matthiessen's role as a delegate to the Progressive Party Convention and as a trustee of the Samuel Adams School of Social Studies which, they added, was on "the subversive list of the Attorney General's office."

Professor Harry Levin, a colleague of Matthiessen's at Harvard, wrote a letter to the *Times* (April 14, 1950) protesting their coverage of the professor's death:

> The account of the suicide of F. O. Matthiessen in your issue of April 2, perhaps because it was printed as a news story rather than as an obituary, did less than justice to a distinguished man of letters. Thus it mentioned various left-wing affiliations, but made no mention of the numerous literary and academic honors that Professor Matthiessen has received . . .it did not refer to his monumental study of nineteenth century writers, *American Renaissance*.
>
> Mr. Matthiessen's friends, sharing his respect for the complexities of human personality, are far from certain that he undertook what he himself called "this desperate act" in order to provide Mr. F. and his colleagues with a political object-lesson.

Matthiessen's homosexuality was not acknowledged in any of the articles, nor was his relationship with Cheney nor his despair over

Cheney's death. The *Dictionary of American Biography,* which acknowl-
edges Matthiessen's friendship with Cheney as "the closest personal
relationship of his life," trivializes the loss Matthiessen felt at
Cheney's death by stating that his "last years were saddened by the
death of his father, the death of Russell Cheney and Phelps Putnam
and Theodore Spencer." Certainly all these deaths affected
Matthiessen, but surely Cheney's death had the most profound and
wrenching effect.[44]

Other accounts ignore the substantive aspect of his relationship
with Cheney, simply stating "Matthiessen was unmarried,"[45] or describing him as "The balding, soft spoken scholar who lived alone in
bachelor's quarters."[46] By merely stating "He was a bachelor,"[47]
Matthiessen's lifelong relationship with Cheney is invalidated. Many
of us are all too aware that this failure to acknowledge gay relationships, even life-long relationships, contributes to the invisibility of
lesbians and gay men and that it also allows people to analyze
Matthiessen's suicide without all the most pertinent information. To
refuse to see a man who had experienced fantasies of jumping out of
windows if his lover died, as living out these fantasies through his
suicide, is to deny the most profound motivation in his death. It is
clear that Matthiessen's failure to find a comfortable peace with his
homosexuality troubled him after Cheney's death and was a factor in
his suicide. Kenneth Lynn sensed Matthiessen's discomfort with his
homosexuality as a student in his classes:

> Since there was such a strong autobiographical element in his
> criticism, I was struck by Matthiessen's silence, in his lectures and
> tutorial conversations, on the subject of homosexuality in Ameri-
> can literature. His comments on Whitman's interest in young male
> beauty were singularly guarded and inadequate, while the blatant
> case of Hart Crane obviously made him uncomfortable. The con-
> clusion I drew from this at the time, and have subsequently had no
> reason to doubt, was that Matthiessen's own sex life was a guilt-
> ridden horror to him. So full of revulsion was he that he could
> barely pronounce the word homosexuality, let alone release his
> feelings through candid discussions.[48]

Matthiessen's suicide is clearly a complex death spurred on by a
combination of several unfortunate factors. While it does not provide us with a clear-cut case of a suicide caused by the singular factor
of the loss of a loved one, it provides an excellent example of how
this factor may contribute to a person's suicidal feelings. Statistics
indicate that the risk of suicide is 2.5 times higher for a widow
during the first year after her husband's death and 1.5 times higher

during the second, third and fourth years.[49] While no statistics are available on the gay population in a similar situation, the mere fact that a stable sexual relationship is discontinued is evidence enough for increased risk of depression and suicide. "When any aspect of sexuality is lost or diminished significantly," one researcher wrote, "the probability of premature death and/or suicide increases."[50] The loss of a lover is not uncommon among gay men and lesbians. An increased awareness of the ramifications of such loss and the development of appropriate support services for the "widows" will be a deterrent to future suicides.

7.

Ending Gay Suicide

*"Women Wisdom: We gotta keep each other alive any way we can 'cause
nobody else is goin' do it."*
—Quoted in *The Faggots & Their Friends Between Revolutions*,
by Larry Mitchell (Ithaca: Calamus, 1977)

We cannot realistically expect to be able to prevent all lesbians and
gay men from attempting or committing suicide. The broad range
of motivations that spur a person to suicide are too complex and too
much a part of the human psyche to ever be completely eradicated.
As long as human society exists, some people will inevitably choose
suicide as an escape from living. Thus for all people—gay, bisexual,
heterosexual—suicide will continue to be an option.

Suicides that are motivated by factors specifically linked to one's
homosexuality *can* be diminished, and the factors that contribute to
the gay community's high risk for depression and suicide can become less influential. These require, however, a tremendous amount
of work at all levels of society, in suicide intervention, postvention
and prevention.

INTERVENTION

Most people experiencing distress that is intense enough to cause
serious suicidal feelings need immediate help. This is when suicide
intervention takes place. The distinction between suicide prevention
and suicide intervention is between the long-term planning which
will decrease a population's risk for suicide and the immediate services which may deter an individual from taking her or his life. If the
individual is at the peak of crisis, hospitalization may be necessary
until feelings of desperateness abate. For some people, speaking to a
counselor or calling a hotline are enough to prevent them from
hurting themselves. Even if one is able to survive the time of crisis,
that does not mean that the risk for suicide is over. Any person who
comes close to attempting suicide should seriously consider entering
some kind of therapy.

Gay people who are in need of counseling must be careful to find a counselor who is knowledgeable about lesbian or gay male issues and is not homophobic. Most urban areas have a gay-oriented counseling service that can provide psychiatrists, psychologists and social workers, many of whom are themselves lesbians or gay men. If a gay-oriented service is not available, many of the gay churches can refer people to suitable counselors, and feminist health clinics may make referrals to counselors sensitive to the needs of lesbians.

Hotlines and crisis intervention agencies can be a good source of befriending or counseling for suicidal people.[1] Depressed and suicidal lesbians and gay men seem to turn to both specifically gay hotlines (including lesbian and women's hotlines) and suicide or crisis-intervention hotlines. These services have developed in many parts of the country in urban, suburban and rural settings and, while specifically gay services tend to be limited to cities and some college towns, general crisis intervention programs seem to be spread throughout the country.

It is also important that members of the lesbian and gay male communities, as well as the friends and families of gay people, be able to recognize and respond to suicidal feelings and actions. While this book has provided information on specific events which may lead to suicide—such as loss of a job or a lover, blackmail, scandal—people should also be familiar with the direct and indirect clues expressed by suicidal people. For example, many people believe that those who talk about killing themselves rarely actually do attempt suicide. This is not true. Many people who have taken their own lives have warned friends or family through various types of verbal and nonverbal clues, which makes it necessary for all of us to become familiar with the warning signals.[2]

Indirect clues to suicidal feelings include changes in a person's usual mode of behavior such as their sleeping patterns, appetite, daily routines, and mood. More direct clues include the planning of an actual attempt, the acquiring of the tools of suicide (a gun, a knife, or pills, for example), or the sudden distribution of one's personal property to friends ("I won't be needing these records anymore"). Although depression is frequently linked to feelings of suicide, all suicidal people are not depressed in an overt manner. Some display feelings of anxiety, excitement, psychosis and agitation. The person may feel inept, perhaps victimized, unable to deal with the problems and pressures which arise and without the ability to remedy their situation.

It is as important to recognize when a person may be feeling suicidal as it is to respond appropriately and immediately to such feelings. A common misconception many people hold about suicide is that if a person is asked whether she or he is feeling suicidal, they will feel encouraged to kill themselves. Actually, a typical response to such questioning is often a sense of relief accompanied by a lessening of the anxiety surrounding those "hidden" feelings. (For a chart of other misconceptions regarding suicide, see Appendix 3.) It is vital that when a person who feels suicidal speaks to us and shares these feelings, we listen and evaluate the seriousness of the person's condition. People expressing suicidal thoughts must be taken seriously he has been thinking of suicide if that seems to be what they are avoiding stating. Be patient and listen to their thoughts and feelings and do not be fooled by people who maintain that they are no longer feeling suicidal when there are other strong indicators of such feelings. It is important to be supportive to a suicidal person and to help them realize that their pain and problems will abate with time but that suicide is a final, permanent action.

Each of us needs to be familiar with the resources in our area for counseling and providing crisis-intervention support for suicidal people. It is necessary that we monitor these services closely for homophobia and antigay biases and that we feel comfortable referring a suicidal person to these programs. One of the best things we can do for our friends is to put them in touch with trained professionals who can help them—psychiatrists, social workers, clergy—as well as provide them with a support network of friends, relatives, and community members to help them through their crisis. Many suicidal people need to feel integrated into a community or social network in order to begin to recover from their crisis.

POSTVENTION

Work also needs to be done on what is termed "postvention" or the attempt to help people *after* a suicide or suicide attempt. This includes providing support for survivors of a suicide attempt, as well as for the friends and lovers and families of people who have killed themselves. Because studies have shown that people close to the victim experience a serious increase in the risk of suicide themselves during the time after a suicide has occurred, it is essential that proper services and support be provided.[3]

"Widows" of lesbians and gay men who have killed themselves often find themselves in particularly stressful situations. Unless proper wills and legal documents have been prepared, many people find themselves involved in legal turmoil with their late lover's family. Story after story has appeared in the gay press in recent years of women and men who have lost their businesses, homes, possessions, cars or important personal articles after their lover's death because proper attention had not been paid to legal matters. It is clear that such difficulties, on top of the feelings of loss, anger and grief that are already present, may be extremely painful and debilitating for the lover. Unfortunately, the few counseling programs available to help widows and widowers with their feelings of loss may be inaccessible to most lesbians and gay men because of the stress associated with coming out to a primarily nongay group of people.

Lesbians and gay men have, like most people, failed to give considerable attention and planning to how we deal with death—as individuals and as a community. This is certainly understandable for a community which has had to put much energy into mere survival, as well as into the development of specifically lesbian and gay identities and cultures. As our loved ones die, however, it becomes more and more important that we develop rituals and procedures for dealing with death that are appropriate to our community. Some people will certainly believe that there is no reason for a person to plan different kinds of ceremonies, burial procedures or wills because she or he happens to be gay and, in fact, many lesbians and gay men feel very happy with the rituals of their traditional religions and cultures and may be happy to have their biological family make the necessary arrangements. Other people see the need for developing a way of death tailored specifically to the special aspects of being a lesbian or a gay man. Special cemeteries, wills and funeral services are slowly and informally being developed. What is needed most is a careful examination of community needs regarding death and dying and the creation and distribution of information on rituals and death procedures that may be options for us.

Of particular note in these procedures is the memorial service, which has frequently been a community response to a death in the community. When David Brill, a writer at *Gay Community News* in Boston, was found dead, friends and community members experienced a range of feelings of shock, anger, grief and fear. Because of the circumstances surrounding the death, as well as Brill's prominence in the gay community, his death was reported in the Boston newspapers and on television news shows. Members of the community, along with family, friends and local political figures, packed the funeral home for the ceremony, yet many were disturbed that

Brill's commitment to lesbian and gay rights was alluded to only through euphemisms and, in fact, the word "gay" was not spoken at all during the ceremony.[4]

Sensing the strong need for a gay community gathering to deal with his death, friends organized a memorial service ten days after his death. The service included speakers who shared their personal experiences as friends of the deceased, songs, poetry, the awarding of special governmental citations posthumously to Brill from the Massachusetts Senate and the Boston City Council, and an open microphone period, where community members could rise and share their feelings.[5] The service provided a focus for the feelings of members of the community. Friends have continued to mark Brill's death through yearly dinners commemorating his death.

Claudia Scott's friends decided that it was best for them to hold off any community service until four months after her death. Some friends had attended a viewing held shortly after the death, and unstructured get-togethers of friends from Claudia's lesbian writers group and from the community allowed them to share their initial feelings and support one another through the first waves of shock and sadness. The memorial service held in April (Claudia killed herself in December) included music, poetry, readings from Claudia's work, brief personal statements, and a time for community sharing. Claudia's friends felt that the timing of the service was appropriate and allowed them the time to pass through a four-month mourning process that enhanced their ability to plan and carry out such a service.[6]

Other communities have noted the deaths of lesbians and gay men through similar services, as well as visits to the gravesite, small dinners of the friends of the deceased, and silent candlelight vigils. It seems that the determination of the appropriate manner of mourning the death is made usually by those people closest to the deceased. If a person has been prominent in the community—such as Harvey Milk or Jeannette Foster—the community-at-large may need to be provided with a forum for their grief and, in Milk's case, their outrage. If a person has not been prominent in their community, friends and colleagues or coworkers may be the sole priority and can usually together determine the appropriate mechanism for mourning. At some point, a manual that looks at specific death procedures used by local communities will be very helpful.

The way we acknowledge deaths in our communities and our feelings of loss and anger are essential to the continued development of a healthy community. Particularly when a death has come about through suicide, it is vital that friends and lovers are provided with rituals and procedures that allow the feelings to get out. Without the sanctioned supportive process, survivors may tend to repress and deny particularly painful feelings and may, ultimately, develop intense feelings of depression or suicide themselves.

PREVENTION

While some mental health workers believe that self-destructive tendencies are a product of one's life history and psychological condition, it is dangerous to separate mental health issues from social and political factors. Particularly when one is examining the mental health patterns of a minority community, it is vital to acknowledge the connections between societal patterns of oppression and discrimination and the individual's concept of self. Thomas S. Szasz warns against this separation in *The Myth of Mental Illness:*

> The phenomenology of bodily illness is indeed independent of the socio-economic and political character of the society in which it occurs. But this is emphatically not true for the phenomenology of so-called mental illness, whose manifestations depend upon and vary with the educational, economic, religious, social and political character of the individual and the society in which it occurs.[7]

When one examines the mental health problems of any oppressed minority, it is soon apparent that the attitudes of the culture-at-large have placed the individual in a no-win position. The ramifications of bigotry and discrimination need to be addressed as a problem for the healthy functioning of any member of the minority community, but until societal attitudes are changed, discrimination will continue to take its toll. In a classic analysis of oppression, *Black Rage,* William Grier and Price Cobbs document this phenomenon as it occurs in black people in America:

> Mental illness arises from a conflict between the inner drives pushing for individual gratification and the group demands of the external environment. The method of expressing inner needs has developed in contact with and in response to the environment provided by the parents and that segment of the broader society which impinges on the child. It is as if the child takes into himself a part of the world he experiences while quite young and makes that an integral part of his inner self. It is the synthesis of his own personal drives and his early, now incorporated, environment that he subsequently elaborates into his inner self and it is this which is in conflict with the external world.

Something must change—his inner world, the outer world, or both. Too much psychotherapy involves striving only for a change in the inner world and a consequent adaptation to the world outside. Black people cannot abide this and thoughtful therapists know it. A black man's soul can live only if it is oriented toward a change of the social order. A good therapist helps a man change his inner life so that he can more effectively change his outer world.[8]

A more compressed, peak example of the effects of oppression on the mental health of people is provided by victims of the Holocaust. Studies of the experiences of Jews during their imprisonment in the death-camps reveal that suicide was a common response to the terrible mental, physical and spiritual persecution. Dr. Viktor Frankl, in his analysis of his three years in Nazi concentration camps, *Man's Search for Meaning*, wrote, "The thought of suicide was entertained by nearly everyone, if only for a brief time. It was born of the hopelessness of the situation, the constant danger of death looming over us daily and hourly, and the closeness of the deaths suffered by many of the others."[9]

Bruno Bettelheim described the role that the "death drive," as Freud called it, played in these people:

I know that the horrors one was subjected to made one wish for death as a relief; that is, as the life drives recede, the door is opened for the death drive to overpower the individual. That is why the victims could be herded to the gas chambers without resisting: the transport had turned many of them into walking corpses . . .
[The] lack of world concern, as it weakened life drives, reinforced the death tendencies in the Jews, because they felt completely abandoned, felt that nobody else cared, that nobody but they themselves thought they had a right to live.[10]

I cite these examples of racism in the United States and the Holocaust in Europe as clear examples of the effects of extreme hatred, persecution, and threat to life on the individual's ability to function in good health. Confronted with deep fears and threats of violence, people are left with a choice of succumbing or finding a means to cope and survive. While the systematic destruction of people through the Nazi war machine is a uniquely pernicious horror of our times, I believe that the various responses of Holocaust victims to their persecution provide us with clues to the ways people are able to endure the day-to-day suffering wreaked on oppressed minorities in America. The stages of disbelief, anger, resolve and resoluteness which appear in Frankl's portraits of Holocaust victims have their correlates in less immediate but equally destructive forms of annihilation.

That lesbians and gay men have lived with the threat of violence, shame, and societal hatred is no longer difficult to document. Lesbian and gay male historians are uncovering the varied responses of societies to homosexual women and men throughout history.[11] We have been burned as witches, castrated and mutilated, imprisoned in jails, asylums and hospital wards, lobotomized, given shock treatment, murdered by strangers, executed by the state and interned in the same Nazi death-camps Bettelheim and Frankl discuss.

Until now, it has been far too easy for too many people to discount the persecution of lesbians and gay men because of official history's silence about our lives or because a contrived hierarchy of oppression has resulted in the trivializing of the persecution visited on gay people. The threat to life that almost daily faces every lesbian and gay man forces them to make a choice—conscious or unconscious—between annihilation and the struggle for survival.

It is therefore crucial to acknowledge that the root cause of suicide among lesbians and gay men lies in the persecution and oppression which we experience. Our lesbianism or homosexuality is not, in itself, inherently self-destructive. As Sidney Abbott and Barbara Love wrote in *Sappho Was a Right-On Woman:*

> We see that it is not Lesbianism that makes some Lesbians prone to alcoholism, suicide, or drug abuse; it is the self-degradation our society went to such pains to teach us, and which is hammered into us not only by the overwhelming force of public opinion, but specifically by lost jobs, lost homes, and—if we are mothers—by lost children.[12]

Personal testimony by a gay man before the California Legislature's Subcommittee on Medical Education and Health Needs clearly indicates that oppression and discrimination have had a direct effect on this man's mental health:

> I am homosexual; this fact has affected my mental health. I was expelled from a New England prep school just prior to my graduation (after four years there) when my homosexuality was discovered. Two years later, a psychiatrist at the University of Pennsylvania's student health service violated my privileged communication, reporting to the dean that I had sought psychiatric help regarding my homosexual behavior and I was forced to leave Penn. Less than a year later, the San Francisco psychiatrist who

had helped me so much after the previous trauma suicided at least partly because of his inability to cope with his own homosexual feelings. After serving as minister to a Unitarian congregation for seven years, since speaking openly about my sexuality, I have been denied ministerial employment.

These are examples of the kinds of prejudice faced by many homosexuals in our society. I cite the personal examples to demonstrate that my mental health problems, as with many homosexuals, were partly induced by a hostile society. Internally, my sexuality has felt appropriate, comfortable and morally sound; the contrasting attitude of the society produced the conflict in my life.

It is not relevant to assess why my life experiences did not evoke depressive or suicidal behavior in me. However, after four years of intensive contact with persons admitted to San Francisco General Hospital as a consequence of injuries sustained in suicide attempts, it is clear to me that much depression and suicidal behavior results from alienation caused by prejudice in this society.[13]

Recent interpretations of Durkheim's earlier findings on the causes of suicide make clear that the status which lesbians and gay men are granted as societal outcasts is directly related to increased suicide rates. As two doctors have written:

> The greater the strength of social relations in a population, the lower the suicide rate . . .The generalization can be extended by assuming that the strength of social relations is largely a matter of the members conforming to socially sanctioned expectations of behavior or, stated otherwise, conformity to the roles of their various statuses. But whether or not persons conform to roles depends primarily on the compatibility of the roles. If, for example, conformity to one's occupational roles makes it difficult to conform to one's marital roles, the individual is confronted with a roll conflict. Stated another way, he occupies incompatible statuses. This line of reasoning suggests the following generalization: the more members of a population who occupy incompatible statuses, the higher the suicide rate.[14]

It is evident that, until societal attitudes change significantly and one's status as a lesbian or gay man does not produce conflict with one's status as a working person, or parent, or teenager, or any of the many other roles we fill, suicide will continue to plague lesbians and gay men.

This study has documented only one tragic option that people have taken in response to their pain and persecution. Many women and men have not committed suicide but have internalized society's message of hatred and adopted vehement antihomosexual attitudes themselves. We are all aware of the various antigay politicians and public figures who have been arrested for engaging in homosexual activities themselves (often in public restrooms and parks). One can only wonder how these people are able to survive the discrepancy between their sexual desires and their adopted homophobia.

Yet another response to oppression which allows for survival is the feeling of helplessness and ennui which infects a person. Viktor Frankl describes such a response in concentration-camp victims:

> When a man finds that it is his destiny to suffer, he will have to accept his suffering as his task; his single and unique task. He will have to acknowledge the fact that even in suffering he is unique and alone in the universe. No one can relieve him of his suffering or suffer in his place. His unique opportunity lies in the way in which he bears his burden.[15]

Some lesbians and gay men have adopted similar attitudes towards their own suffering and seen their condition as unalterable, hopeless, doomed. Rudy Kikel found this sense of doom evidenced in gay poetry;

> Beside "love" or "camp," the literary tradition of what I should call gay "doom" is the neglected stepsister, the Cinderella of gay male sensibility, always "passing" for something else (the "failure" of love, for instance), little recognized or appreciated even by her *own* . . . And yet gay "doom" may be now the most venerable as it has been to earlier generations the most disreputable of aspects to the gay male sensitivity since World War II, since after all it was presentation of our "doom" which put an end in poetry to gay invisibility . . . and since it bears, more even than our "love" poems or our campiness, marks of the origins of gay oppression in heterosexual confusion.[16]

Still other lesbians and gay men have denied the relevance of their sexuality or opted for assimilation or self-denial and repression. Regardless of the personal responses to the threats targeting the mere existence of lesbianism and male homosexuality, the options have all, until recently, taken a tremendous toll on the mental health of the survivor. Only during the past decade or so have other options become available to gay people which allow for responses to societal oppression which are not directed inward and do not result in self-infecting with self-hatred and self-destructiveness.

The new options came about in the late 1960s, in the context of the struggles of various disenfranchised groups to gain power and self-determination. Throughout the 1950s and early 1960s, lesbians and gay men were beginning to come together to develop a community identity distinct from the stereotypes that had become a part of the opposition. The Stonewall Riots, in 1969, which came about after police staged one of their routine raids on a gay bar in New York City, have attained mythic stature in the gay community. This is because the resistance ignited at the Stonewall Inn, which turned from verbal to violent resistance to police harassment and threats, was the first visible and public unleashing of gay rage. That night lesbians and gay men throughout the world came to realize: "We no longer have to internalize their hatred, feel helpless, repress our love or kill ourselves. We *can* fight back."

The connection between the Stonewall Riots and other movements for social and political change is noted by gay historian John D'Emelio:

> The Stonewall Riot did not create a gay liberation movement out of nothing; the seeds had already started to sprout by the time the police raided the Christopher Street bar. Stonewall was the catalyst that allowed gay women and men to appropriate to themselves the example, insight and inspiration of the radical movements of the 1960s—black power, the new left, the counterculture and, above all, feminism—and take a huge leap forward toward liberation.[17]

The years since Stonewall have seen the launching of a ubiquitous and powerful movement of women and men who are developing increasing options for themselves and increasing awareness of their identities as lesbians and gay men. Whether the work taking place is organizing a demonstration, registering voters, producing a women's music festival, or appearing on a television talk show, the activity is focusing on changing American society and its attitudes towards plurality. These new choices which are available to increasing numbers of lesbians and gay men have created the true alternative to the assimilation and passivity, repression and suicide of the past.

Thus we find ourselves at a particularly exciting and particularly precarious time for lesbians and gay men. More and more women and men are acquiring an identity which, from childhood, we have been taught to despise.[18] This essential contradiction lies at the core of our identities as lesbians and gay men in the 1980s. While more women and men are now publicly or privately identifying themselves as lesbians and gay men than ever before, society is not providing adequate support and services for us as we pass through this rocky period. Furthermore, while we have found an option that grants us a measure of positive attitudes toward ourselves, cultural attitudes have, as yet, changed too little to afford gay people substantial assistance in our struggle to avoid lives that are, on one level, fraught with doubt and self-hatred. Some activists have noted the impressive progress which has been made in bringing male homosexuality and lesbianism into a forum for discussion, yet young lesbians and gay men continue to express the feelings of isolation and conflict which we felt when we were younger. Times are changing, but American society's ability to address the needs of the gay population has not at all kept pace with the degree to which this population has increasingly been asserting itself.

Thus preventing suicide based on factors relating specifically to lesbians and gay men will require further changes—both in society at large and within the gay population. While many activists are unaware of any conscious and clearly-defined agenda of their work for lesbian and gay male liberation and rights, the changes that need to take place to create a community with improved mental health read like the demands issued at a press conference or a march on Washington, D.C.: the elimination of laws which discriminate or persecute lesbians and gay men; the promotion of positive images of the lives of gay people through the media and through the examples of individual lives; the establishment of specific programs and services to meet the health needs of lesbians and gay men.

It may sound idealistic to believe that such changes can take place in our culture or that the changes themselves will bring about an end to suicide motivated by antigay oppression, but in case after case of attempted or completed suicide which we have considered, we have seen how specific pressures served as the spark that ignited the suicidal action. The men who killed themselves when arrested on "morals charges" could not have had very positive feelings about themselves prior to their arrests; the threat of legal action and all its ramifications proved too much for them to handle. Only when and if homosexuality is seen as a viable and positive option for women and men and is truly accepted and integrated into all aspects of society, will the gay community be healthier, happier and safer.

There are also efforts that need to be made within the gay community which will serve to strengthen the lesbian and gay male population. Because the gay community is so ill-defined (people still debate the validity of the concept of a gay community) and so anarchistic in nature, it is impossible to hold individuals or organizations accountable for directing the priorities of the community.

Thus it is difficult to effect specific changes in the community or dictate a new direction. Still, if lesbians and gay men can come to see their community's mental health as a priority, specific work needs to be accomplished. The conscious creation of support systems, "families," friendship networks must take place. Because so many lesbians and gay men find themselves estranged from their biological families and because none of us has been raised to see community building and relationship building (outside of heterosexual marriage) as a valuable skill and activity, too many lesbians and gay men drift about with little or no integration into social and support networks. Recently, increased attention has been given by the community to this kind of work and such efforts need to escalate.

Other kinds of intracommunity work that need to be done include the rooting out of all forms of oppressive discrimination within the community—sexism, racism, ageism, classism, anti-Semitism and the oppression of the disabled. To many readers this may sound like a laundry list of "politically correct" target areas for the community, but it is essential that we each understand that discrimination of all kinds takes its toll in mental health. Ending racism requires more than affirmative action and quotas from the community, it requires substantial changes in all of us on a deep and profound personal level. Because the majority of gay people experience multiple forms of discrimination based on their identities as women, people of color, working class and poor people, Jews, or physically challenged people, any attempt to eradicate homophobia and end suicide brought about by antigay oppression must include substantial work within the gay community to combat all other forms of oppression.

The specific needs of lesbians and gay men who are young and old must be looked at by the community. Many gay men believe that, after a certain age (perhaps as young as 40), they will no longer be sexually desirable and then proceed to conclude that their life will soon no longer be worth living. Age discrimination against both youth and elderly is rife in the community, and young people coming out in their schools and older people who are "single" are two populations which experience specific and serious pressures. While groups of older lesbians and gay men and of lesbian and gay youth have begun to form, until a broader integration of people of all ages into the larger community is achieved, the practice of ageism will continue to undermine the mental health of large portions of our community.

Another responsibility that each gay person needs to assume is responsibility for "coming out" as much as is possible. It is our individual right and duty to determine for ourselves what degree of openness we can personally afford to achieve, based on our own needs and experiences, the kind of community we live and work in, the status of our legal rights, the support systems we have in our lives. No one can determine for any of us just how open we can really afford to be except ourselves. It is time, however, for the blatant denial of our identities as gay men and lesbians to be challenged on the personal level. We each need to work to eliminate the deception and masquerade many lesbians and gay men live with. Hiding our homosexuality through deceptive marriages, for example, may have been appropriate in the sixties and before but no longer should be condoned. If we cannot be open about our sexuality and our personal primary relationships, we should attempt to be private only about our lives. To resort to lying and faked relationships is dangerous for ourselves and for other gay people who are then often led to see coworkers, politicians, movie stars, and friends who are gay as heterosexual. This increases the invisibility of the community and creates fewer positive images of unmarried men and women in our culture.

We must realize that the rise of the reactionary Right during the past five years has brought a change to our agenda of working towards a society that accepts different ways of loving and differing attitudes towards sexuality. As conservative forces have increasingly asserted themselves at all levels of government, gay people find themselves included with blacks, Jews, women, Hispanics, Asians, the elderly and the disabled, as targets for victimization and increased persecution. Any reader of the gay press is aware of the increase in violence against lesbians and gay men and the invasion of our bars, meeting places, churches, businesses and homes by antigay gangs, military personnel, and police officers at a rate which we have not seen since before 1969. Many activists have wondered whether the growing tide of oppression would force lesbians and gay men to quickly retreat underground—back to the days of the closet, the pseudonym, the cover-up marriage.

Despite these fearful predictions, I believe we are seeing the development of a strong resistance to the increased repression of our times. Lesbian and gay male organizations continue to swell in number and membership and are becoming increasingly adept at developing effective strategies to fight the Right. This may be because we are more aware of the alternative to resistance and of the expense that a life of denial would bring us. Our identities as lesbians and gay men are stronger than ever, and the core of gay people who have worked through the bulk of their passivity, self-hatred and fear serve as inspirations to other gay people just emerging from the closet.

Continued resistance, therefore, is the major work of suicide prevention that needs to continue within our community of lesbians and gay men. Statistics are not available to indicate whether the past years of the movement for lesbian and gay male liberation have resulted in creating a climate where fewer gay people become desperate and unhappy. One might expect that there is an inverse relationship between the development of pride and the feelings of self-destructiveness in an oppressed minority. As Sally Casper of the Samaritans of Boston said, "Since it doesn't help to be a part of a minority that is not socially respected, the gay rights movement certainly is helping to change that. I expect the movement will continue to make more and more people happier with themselves."[19]

Thus we find that ending suicides brought about by factors related to being a lesbian or a gay man is a complex and multifaceted task. While service providers must become trained in the special needs of the lesbian and gay male population, their work takes place during the actual suicidal crisis. Our ultimate goal is to prevent people from ever reaching the crisis stage. This aspect of suicide prevention is long-range and requires tremendous changes in the gay community, as well as in society at large. A society that forces a gay person into suicide by making life unbearable and ugly, by attempting to portray all lesbians and gay men as sick, evil and unworthy of life, and by conspiracy to eliminate all of us from the world—by our own hands, if necessary—is a society that engages in coercive mass murder.

Suicide among lesbians and gay men is not an isolated, personal action. It is just one part of a strategy of genocide against lesbians and gay men and thus requires much more than mere assistance to individuals in crisis. Health providers may do their work well, but unless politicians, editors, church officials and educators see the impact of their actions on the lives of lesbians and gay men, the problems of the gay community in regard to suicide will continue. Ending gay suicide requires an end to the discrimination, hatred, violence and trivialization used against lesbians and gay men; ultimately, it requires a strategy for social and political change that will transform our society radically for all of us.

APPENDIXES

Appendix 1
SAPPHO'S "SUICIDE"

That Sappho is known today as an important poet or as a lesbian is an amazing testament to her talents. Historians and literary critics, predominantly men, have manipulated the sparse details of her biography during the twenty-six centuries since she lived on the island of Lesbos in the Aegean Sea. As they wrestled with the burden of evaluating a woman of indisputable talent who clearly revealed erotic passion for other women, various "misinformation" found its way into her biography—including her now reknowned suicide leap from the Leucadian cliffs. Sappho is included here, not because she is the first prominent lesbian "suicide" in history, but because she is an example of the manner in which the assumption of hysteria and self-destructiveness as primary characteristics of lesbians has permitted historians and critics to invent biographical information for which there is no factual evidence.

We know very little about Sappho's life. The biographical information known to contemporary historians is limited to details gleaned from the fragments that remain of her work and from the writings of classical authors (who were often influenced by their own biases). We know that she was writing poetry at the age of 17 in the town of Mitylene on the island of Lesbos. She spent several years in what may have been political exile on the island of Sicily. On returning to Lesbos, she gathered women about her, teaching them poetry, music and dance and formed what one writer referred to as the first women's club.[1] We also know of her love for several women, including Erinna and Atthis. We do not know much more.[2]

The manipulation that Sappho's biography has undergone since her death illustrates quite clearly the dilemma facing literary critics and historians: What does one say about a superior poet who was clearly a lover of her own sex? Many writers simply ignored the strong evidence that indicates that Sappho loved women. Joseph Addison, writing in *The Spectator* in 1711, did not mention her love for women at all.[3] Others did their best to rationalize her seeming distaste for men. Arthur Weigall, the modern writer who has, perhaps, manipulated Sappho's biography most clearly to suit his own ends, readily admits in his *Sappho of Lesbos* (1932) that the poet "does not seem to have displayed any particular interest in the opposite sex."[4] Weigall, however, somehow feels compelled to defend Sappho from the assumption that she was a "man-hater":

It was not that she disliked men—for it is to be remembered
that she died in the end for love of a man; but it can readily be
understood that she must have found the young warriors, hot
from the war, a little too rough for her, habituated as she was by
the circumstances of the time to feminine society.[5]

Other writers have acknowledged her lesbianism but concluded
that, despite being "damned" by this inclination, Sappho remained
celibate throughout her life. Denys Page, in *Sappho and Alcaeus*
(1955), wrote "that she was addicted to the perversion which the
modern world names after her native island." Page continues,

> To the further question—so often propounded, so seldom con-
> sidered without prejudice—whether evidence for practice as well
> as inclination is to be found in the fragments of Sappho's poetry, a
> negative answer must be returned. It is at least probable that
> Lesbos in her lifetime was notorious for the perverse practice of its
> women; but in all that remains of Sappho's poetry there is not a
> word which connects herself or her companions with them.[6]

Dolores Klaich, in her landmark study of attitudes towards lesbianism, *Woman + Woman* (1974), discusses another very popular
way of dealing with Sappho's sexuality: by making her bisexual
(always preferable to unrepentent lesbianism!). Klaich traces the
development of this theory from the writings of the Roman poet
Ovid, who in one work wrote that Sappho's poems "constituted a
veritable course of instruction in female homosexuality," while in
another work launched the myth of Sappho's love for a man and
subsequent suicide. If we are to believe the story, Sappho at age
fifty-five fell wildly in love with Phaon, a twenty year old ferryman.
Phaon did not share Sappho's amorous feelings and, after pursuing
him throughout the Aegean, the poet climbed to the top of a cliff in
Leucadia and, heartbroken, threw herself into the waters below.[7]

Critics and historians have dealt with Ovid's tale of Sappho's late-
in-life foray into heterosexual love and subsequent suicide in a
variety of ways. William Mure, in *A Critical History of the Language and
Literature of Ancient Greece* (1854), believed that the "habits" of the
poet seemed to support Ovid's legend. He described Sappho as
"impelled by a fervid temperament and the impatience of disappointed love" and thus felt comfortable verifying the Leucadian
leap.[8] Others, such as Weigall, seem determined to provide all the
evidence needed to prove Ovid's story, despite the obvious lack of
any substantial biographical evidence.[9]

Some writers have clearly refuted the suicide story. As early as

1850, William Smith in the *New Classical Dictionary* insisted that "this well-known story vanishes at the first approach of criticism." Smith cites the fact 'that "the name of Phaon does not occur in one of Sappho's poems and there is no evidence that it was mentioned in her poems" to relegate the story to the realm of legend.[10]

John Arthur Thomas Lloyd, in his book *Sappho: Life and Work* (1910), sums up the many myths surrounding Sappho's life:

> Sappho's husband, her supposed lack of beauty, her amours, her *role* as instructor, her Bacchic revels, her pursuit of Phaon— over all and each of these exploited suppositions the greatest doubt continues to hang. Finally, the very existence of Phaon and the actuality of the leap itself belong, not improbably, to the realm of legend.[11]

Over the past 2,600 years, as different cultures have attempted to come to terms with Sappho's life and poetry, their attitudes toward independent women and toward lesbianism influenced their perspective. As T. G. Johnson wrote in *Sappho: The Lesbian* (1899), "All opinions formed by men on women are apt to be intense and exaggerated, and most women who have presumed to help forward the progress of their sex have almost always and in all ages been uniformly misunderstood if not slandered and reviled."[12]

Dolores Klaich documents cultural attitudes towards lesbianism which resulted in the ridicule, censure and burnings of Sappho's work. The latter took place c. A.D. 380 in the Eastern Roman Empire and in the eleventh century in the West. For this detailed study, see Dolores Klaich: *Woman + Woman: Attitudes Toward Lesbianism* (New York: William Morrow, 1974).

Appendix 2
RECENT "CHRISTIAN" LITERATURE EXPLOITING GAY SUICIDE

Dealing honestly with gay suicide has been made more difficult during recent years by conservative and religious forces which have manipulated and exaggerated the statistics on gay people and suicide and used them inappropriately for their own political ends. Insisting that homosexuality is, by its very nature, a lethal condition, an impressive collection of New Right literature has developed around this subject.

These writers believe that half of all suicides are a result of homosexuality. While this figure is quoted in book after book, nowhere have I located adequate documentation for (or even an adequate attempt to document) this information. Tim LaHaye, in his book *The Unhappy Gays* wrote:

> One writer claims that 50 percent of the suicides in America can be attributed to homosexuality. In my book *How to Win Over Depression*, I reported that the minimum number of estimated suicides in America runs between 50,000 and 70,000 annually. If that writer is right, from 25,000 to 35,000 homosexuals commit suicide each year in the greatest country on earth. If these statistics are valid, then the suicide rate among the homosexual community is twelve to fourteen times greater than that of the straight community.[1]

In her book *The Anita Bryant Story: The Survival of Our Nation's Families and the Threat of Militant Homosexuals*, Anita Bryant claims to quote statistics which indicate "50% of all suicides and homicides in big cities can be attributed to homosexuals."[2]

The theoretical connection of homosexuality with morbidity and lethality has roots in the late nineteenth century but is undergoing interesting new developments at the present time. Paul Cameron, an associate professor of psychology at Fuller Theological Seminary Graduate School of Psychology and a leading conservative writer on these matters, has even extended the connection between homosexuality and lethality further back in time and manipulated history to fit his political end. Cameron travels back to classical Greece to document the "lethal theme" of homosexuality by stating that, "Companies of homosexual warriors were assembled because it was believed that they made better killers." What is even more outrageous is his manipulation of the Holocaust by insisting that there were "disproportionate numbers of homosexuals in [Roehm's] storm troopers" and "the *Capos* in the German concentration camps were apparently disproportionately homosexual." He insists that "when a really gory murder is committed, police experience suggests that disproportionately frequently it is a homosexual killing." This leads Cameron to conclude "the narcissistic homosexual is apparently better suited to take human life—whether his own or another's."[3]

There are strong connections between the association of homosexuality and morbidity with the assumption that lesbians and gay men are childless and cannot create human life. Once accepting this incorrect statement (which assumes sterility and sexual dysfunction), many people have gone on to conclude that we need to "convert" others to our "evil ways" and thus we prey on helpless children to spirit them into homosexual practices. Recent writings on this subject also connect lesbianism to what they define as "the taking of human life" (which we know as a medical procedure called abortion). Cameron cites a study that concludes, "Those females who claimed to have obtained an abortion (12% of our sample) five times more frequently than non-aborters claimed a less-than-exclusively-heterosexual orientation." He connects this to another aspect of the study where "males who claimed that they had killed or participated in killing other humans (20% of our sample) four times more frequently claimed a less-than-exclusively-heterosexual orientation." This allows Cameron to conclude that, "As the taking of human life is such a vital part of any ethic, the social interest may be sufficiently involved to suppress homosexuality on this count alone."[4]

Thus fundamentalist religious writers and conservative scholars accumulate statistics appropriate to their thesis that lesbians and gay men—by nature—are associated with morbidity and lethality. This information is used, time after time, to suit their political goals. To drive fear of homosexuality into people's minds they cite studies which implicate us in murder, suicide, abortion and euthanasia (the latter two issues being highly charged among today's fundamentalists). By exaggerating the fact of gay suicide and failing to analyze the root causes of unhappiness among some lesbians and gay men, they are able to conclude: "Even if we cut the figures in half, making the suicide rate six or seven times greater than that of straights, it would prove my point—that 'gay' isn't gay!"[5] This is used to persuade as yet unacknowledged homosexuals to stay in the closet or seek conversion counseling. Throughout conservative literature of the past 20 years, ignorant "experts" have hammered home that homosexuality *is* sickness:

Homosexuality, by definition, is not healthy or wholesome . . . The homosexual person, at best, will be unhappier and more unfulfilled than the normal person. There are emotional and physical consequences to this protracted state of mental dissatisfaction. At worst, the homosexual person will die younger and suffer emotional, mental and physical illness more often than the normal person. The natural history of the homosexual person seems to be one of frigidity, impotence, broken personal relationships, psychosomatic disorders, alcoholism, paranoia psychosis and suicide.[6]

The most dangerous aspect of the insistence of certain groups and individuals that homosexuality *is* sick is that it encourages certain people with some degree of power to behave less than responsibly with lesbian or gay male clients. One particularly disturbing abuse of the role of the pastoral counselor, printed below, summarizes the end result of these antigay attitudes:

Less than two months ago I was told by a sincere Christian counselor that it would be "better" to "repent and die," even if I had to kill myself, than to go on living and relating to others as a homosexual. (A friend of mine, told something similar by a well-intentioned priest, did just that.)[7]

Thus we see how conservative forces, linking homosexuality inherently with morbidity, are able to proceed to encourage suicide among lesbians and gay men, urge sterilization for lesbians, and advocate the death penalty for people discovered to have engaged in homosexual activities.

Appendix 3
COMMON MISCONCEPTIONS ABOUT SUICIDE

FALSE	TRUE
1. People who talk about suicide rarely commit suicide.	1. People who commit suicide have given some clue or warning of intent. Suicide threats and attempts must be taken seriously.
2. The tendency toward suicide is inherited and passed on from one generation to another.	2. Suicide does not "run in families." It has no characteristic genetic quality.
3. The suicidal person wants to die and feels there is no turning back.	3. Suicidal persons most often reveal ambivalence about living versus dying and frequently call for help immediately following the suicide attempt.
4. Everyone who commits suicide is depressed.	4. Although depression is often associated with suicidal feelings, not all people who kill themselves are obviously depressed: Some are anxious, agitated, psychotic, organically impaired, or wish to escape their life situation.
5. There is very little correlation between alcoholism and suicide.	5. Alcoholism and suicide often go hand in hand; that is, a person who commits suicide is often also an alcoholic.
6. A person who commits suicide is mentally ill.	6. Although persons who commit suicide were often distraught, upset or depressed, many of them would not have been medically diagnosed as mentally ill.
7. A suicide attempt means that the attempter will always entertain thoughts of suicide.	7. Often, a suicide attempt is made during a particularly stressful period. If the remainder of that period can be appropriately managed, then the attempter can go on with life.

8. If you ask a client directly, "Do you feel like killing yourself?" this will lead him or her to make a suicide attempt.

8. Asking a client directly about suicidal intent will often minimize the anxiety surrounding the feeling and act as a deterrent to the suicidal behavior.

9. Suicide is more common among lower socioeconomic groups than than elsewhere in our society.

9. Suicide crosses all socioeconomic groups and no one group is more susceptible than another.

10. Suicidal persons rarely seek medical help.

10. In retrospective studies of committed suicide, more than half had sought medical help within six months preceding the suicide.

(Courtesy of The Samaritans of Boston)

Appendix 4
COUNSELING SUICIDAL LESBIANS AND GAY MEN THROUGH HOTLINES

Telephone hotlines may be a tremendous resource to depressed and suicidal people. Located in most urban centers as well as many suburban and rural communities, they may be able to provide the comfort and reassurance needed to survive a suicidal crisis. Many of these hotlines are listed at the front of telephone directories or may be located by contacting a local hospital, police station or health clinic.

While it appears vital that crisis intervention volunteers be screened for antigay attitudes and trained to meet the specific needs of lesbians and gay men in crisis, this does not always occur. The Samaritans hotline in Boston carefully screens its phone volunteers for homophobic attitudes and they have a class for phone volunteers that specifically focuses on gay concerns. Sally Casper, co-director of the Samaritans, explained that, "Volunteers need to know that gay people can be just like people who are not gay. A person's homosexuality doesn't have to be an issue; the emotions are often the same. We also make sure that our volunteers don't have the idea that homosexuality is a stage of 'incomplete emotional development.' That is a clear put-down."[1]

The crisis intervention hotline of Life Crisis Service, Inc. of St. Louis also screens workers and will not accept volunteers who harbor biases against gay people. Half their training sessions on "Sexuality-Related Calls" are devoted to gay issues. The session includes viewing a documentary film which contains a "consciousness-raising tone," personal sharings by trainers who are gay, open discussion on various issues about being gay and about the needs of gay callers, and resources in the St. Louis community for lesbians and gay men.[2]

Often hotlines which are not specifically oriented towards lesbians and gay men receive calls from people who are hesitant to identify themselves as gay. Asking if the caller is gay may be awkward for the phone staffer and may cause stress in the caller as well but hotlines find ways to circumvent these problems. Sally Casper said, "If a caller is being very careful to avoid pronouns, right away I'm alerted that the lover they're talking about is possibly of the same sex and I'm careful not to presume that it is of the opposite sex. Sometimes in that situation I'll say, 'How did you meet him or her?' If they're gay, it conveys that it would be acceptable to me and people tend to open up more."[3]

Lesbian and gay hotlines generally report few phone calls from overtly suicidal people but tend to include specific training sessions on suicide because many of their volunteers are most concerned about handling such calls. An advocate at the Gay Hotline in Ann Arbor, Michigan, says that, while callers may not make references to being suicidal, "If I think a caller is suicidal, I mention it to get it into the open." Their hotline staff is provided with a four-hour training session which discusses theories of suicidal ideation, followed by taped role-plays and discussion of the tapes involving depressed and suicidal callers.[4] The Lincoln Gay Crisis and Referral Line in Lincoln, Nebraska, includes similar training which emphasizes crisis intervention and suicide and is followed by monthly sessions that focus on specific topics. Larry Wiseblood, coordinator of the hotline, said, "We deal with these topics often because peer counselors see this as their toughest role."[5]

Staffers at the Gay Hotline in Ann Arbor report few phone calls by overtly suicidal lesbians and gay men but have found that there are signals which a caller may give that might indicate suicidal tendency, including "indirect statement, vocal tone, level of vocal energy, silent periods, refusal to try to help self move from problem to positive goal."[6] New York's Gay Switchboard recommends referring all suicide calls immediately to a professional such as the nearest hospital and, if an attempt has been made, the volunteer is requested to find out the caller's name, address and phone number and pass it along to the police who may respond with emergency treatment. They further caution their volunteers: "Remember: When dealing with the police department, do not use the word 'gay.' There have been complaints about lack of response and even outright hostility when the word 'gay' was mentioned."[7]

Thus, on one level, counselors, hotline volunteers and staffers and medical professionals must be able to provide quality treatment to depressed and suicidal people in general and lesbians and gay men specifically. Training sessions on the special needs of the gay population must be given to all staffers at crisis intervention programs and instruction on counseling suicidal people must be provided for staffers at lesbian and gay hotlines. Both services must provide appropriate referrals to counselors and other professionals who can respond in a helpful way to desperate gay people.[8]

NOTES

Chapter 1
THE MYTH AND THE FACT OF GAY SUICIDE, pages 1–24

The following works have formed the basis for my understanding of the place of lesbians and gay men throughout history as discussed in this chapter: Jonathan Katz: *Gay American History: Lesbians and Gay Men in the U.S.A.* (New York: Thomas Y. Crowell, 1976); *Frontiers: A Journal of Women Studies,* "Lesbian History Issue," vol. IV, no. 3 (Fall, 1979) (Boulder: Women's Studies Program, University of Colorado); Jeffrey Weeks: *Coming Out: Homosexual Politics in Britain from the Nineteenth Century to the Present* (London: Quartet Books, 1977); Lillian Faderman: *Surpassing The Love of Men: Romantic Friendships and Love Between Women from the Renaissance to the Present* (New York: William Morrow, 1981); Carroll Smith-Rosenberg: "The Female World of Love and Ritual: Relations Between Women in Nineteenth-Century America" in *Signs,* vol. I, no. 1 (Fall, 1975), 1-29; Vern L. Bullough: *Homosexuality: A History* (New York: New American Library, 1979); Joseph Interrante: "From the Puritans to the Present: 350 Years of Lesbian and Gay History in Boston," in *Gay Jubilee: A Guidebook to Gay Boston—Its History and Resources,* Neuma Crandall, Richard Burns and Eric Rofes, eds. (Boston: Lesbian and Gay Task Force of Jubilee 350, 1980); and Barbara Grier and Coletta Reid: *Lesbian Lives: Biographies of Women from The Ladder* (Baltimore: Diana Press, 1976).

[1] Weeks: *Coming Out,* 12.

[2] A. Alvarez: *The Savage God* (London: Weidenfeld and Nicholson, 1971), 46.

[3] John Winthrop: *History of New England,* vol. 2, 324, as quoted in Katz: *Gay American History,* 22.

[4] *Calendar of [Dutch] Historical Manuscripts, as quoted in Katz: Gay American History,* 22–23.

[5] J. Hammond Trumbull: *The True-Blue Laws of Connecticut and New-Haven* (Hartford: American Pub. Co., 1879), 201. Quoted in Katz: *Gay American History,* 23.

[6] Emile Durkheim: *Suicide* (New York: Free Press, 1951), 327–329; and Edwin S. Shneidman: "Suicide" in Edwin S. Shneidman, ed.: *Death: Current Perspectives* (Palo Alto, CA: Mayfield, 1980), 427.

[7] Durkheim: *Suicide,* 323.

[8] Bullough: *Homosexuality: A History,* 7.

[9] Havelock Ellis and J. A. Symonds: *Sexual Inversion* (London: 1897), as quoted in Interrante: "From the Puritans to the Present . . . ," 27.

[10] For a discussion of these friendships see Smith-Rosenberg: "The Female World of Love and Ritual," and Faderman: *Surpassing the Love of Men.* Also see Blanche Wiesen Cook: "Female Support Networks and Political Activism: Lillian Wald, Crystal Eastman, Emma Goldman," *Chrysalis,* no. 3 (1977), 43–61.

[11] Interrante: "From the Puritans to the Present . . . ," 22.

12 Don Rickey, Jr.: *Forty Miles a Day on Beans and Hay* (Norman: University of Oklahoma, 1963), 170–171, as quoted in Katz: *Gay American History,* 509.

13 Sigmund Freud, "The Psychogenesis of a Case of Female Homosexuality," *International Journal of Psycho-Analysis* (London), vol. I, no. 2 (1920), 125–127. Quoted in Katz: *Gay American History,* 156.

14 Josephine Donovan: "The Unpublished Love Poems of Sarah Orne Jewett," *Frontiers,* vol. IV., no. 3 (Fall, 1979), 27.

15 Interrante: "From the Puritans to the Present . . . ," 15–17.

16 Quoted in Edward Carpenter: *The Intermediate Sex* (London: George Allen & Unwin Ltd., 1908), 118, 158.

17 Dr. R. v. Krafft-Ebing: *Psychopathia Sexualis* (Stuttgart: Enke, 1889), 216–219, as quoted in John Addington Symonds: *Studies in Sexual Inversion* (Privately printed, 1928), 152.

18 Quoted in Edward Carpenter: *The Intermediate Sex,* 139.

19 Weeks: *Coming Out,* 27.

20 *Ibid.*

21 Phyllis Grosskurth: *Havelock Ellis* (New York: Knopf, 1980), 185.

22 Carpenter: *The Intermediate Sex,* 13.

23 Symonds: *Studies in Sexual Inversion,* 120.

24 Emile Durkheim: *Suicide* (New York: Free Press, 1951).

25 Max Marcuse: "Suicide and Sexuality," *The Journal of Sexology and Psychanalysis,* vol. I (January-December, 1923), 184.

26 W. A. O'Connor: "Some Notes on Suicide," *British Journal of Medical Psychology,* vol. 21, pt. 3 (1948), 228.

27 Joost Meerloo: *Suicide and Mass Suicide* (New York: Grune & Stratton, 1962), 57.

28 Jeannette Foster: *Sex Variant Women in Literature* (Baltimore: Diana Press, 2nd ed. 1975), 150.

29 Foster's index alone lists 32 references to suicide or suicide attempts, and a reading of the book reveals many references to suicide which have not been included in the index.

30 Foster: *Sex Variant Women in Literature,* 114.

31 Foster: *Sex Variant Women in Literature,* 239.

32 Ann Aldrich: *We Two Won't Last* (New York: Fawcett, 1963), 111. Being sufficiently ignorant of filmlore, I hesitate to correct Aldrich. A reading of Vito Russo's well-researched history of homosexuals in film, *The Celluloid Closet* (New York: Harper & Row, 1981), indicates that *Olivia* and *Pit of Loneliness* were the same movie. Russo writes, "Jacqueline Audry's *Olivia* (1951) was given a sensational release in the United States as *Pit of Loneliness* (1954)." Russo gives no indication that the suicide of a lesbian takes place in the film.

Russo also discusses the two versions of *Maedchen in Uniform,* one including a suicide at the finale and one without. See *The Celluloid Closet,* 56–58 and 102–103. B. Ruby Rich discusses the manipulation of the finale and the suicide in an extremely insightful and well-researched article, *"Maedchen in Uniform:* From Repressive Tolerance to Erotic Liberation," in *Jump Cut,* no. 24/25, 44–50.

33 Vito Russo: *The Celluloid Closet,* 261–262.

34 Donald Webster Cory: *The Homosexual in America* (New York: Paperback Library Edition, 1963), 98.

35 "The Homosexual: Newly Visible, Newly Understood," *Time Magazine* (October 31, 1969), 61.

36 Mart Crowley: *The Boys in the Band* (New York: Dell, 1968), 181.

37 William J. Helmer: "New York's Middle-Class Homosexuals," *Harper's Magazine* (March, 1963), 89.

38 Faubion Bowers: "Homosex: Living the Life," *Saturday Review* (February 12, 1972), 28.

39 Amariah Brigham: "Statistics of Suicides in the United States," *American Journal of Insanity,* vol. I (1844), 225–234.

40 Jerome A. Motto, M.D.: "Suicide and Suggestibility—The Role of the Press," *American Journal of Psychiatry,* vol. 124, no. 2 (August, 1967), 252–256.

41 Dr. George Weinberg: *Society and the Healthy Homosexual* (Garden City, N. Y.: Doubleday/Anchor, 1973), 21.

42 Cory: *The Homosexual in America,* 98.

43 Aldrich: *We Two Won't Last,* 111.

44 Del Martin and Phyllis Lyon: *Lesbian/Woman* (New York: Bantam, 1972), 27.

45 E. S. Sheidman and N. L. Farberow: "Suicide—The Problem and its Magnitude," *Dept. of Medicine and Surgery Medical Bulletin* (1961), 1–111.

46 Franklyn Nelson, Norman Farberow and Douglas MacKinnon: "The Certification of Suicide in 11 Western States: An Inquiry Into the Validity of Reported Suicide Rates," *Suicide and Life Threatening Behaviors,* vol. 8, no. 2 (Summer, 1978), 75.

47 Erwin Stengel: *Suicide and Attempted Suicide* (New York: Penguin, 1964).

48 Walter Gore: "Sex, Marital Status and Suicide," *Journal of Health and Social Behavior,* vol. 13, no. 2 (June, 1972), 204–213.

49 Alan P. Bell and Martin S. Weinberg: *Homosexualities* (New York: Simon and Schuster, 1978).

50 Bell and Weinberg: *Homosexualities,* 22.

51 Bell and Weinberg: *Homosexualities,* 207.

52 Marcel T. Saghir and Eli Robins: *Male and Female Homosexuality: A Comprehensive Investigation* (Baltimore: Williams & Wilkins, 1973).

53 Marcel T. Saghir, M.D., Eli Robins, M.D., Bonnie Walbran and Kathye A. Gentry: "Homosexuality IV," *American Journal of Psychiatry,* vol. 127, no. 2 (August, 1970), 152.

54 Karla Jay and Allen Young: *The Gay Report: Lesbians and Gay Men Speak Out About Sexual Experiences & Lifestyles* (New York: Summit, 1979).

55 Jay and Young: *The Gay Report,* 729–731.

56 Bell and Weinberg: *Homosexualities,* 162, 166, 374.

57 Jay and Young: *The Gay Report,* 130.

58 Jay and Young: *The Gay Report,* 63.

59 U. S. Department of Health, Education and Welfare: "Mortality from Selected Causes by Marital Status," U. S. Part A. in *Vital and Health Statistics,* National Center for Health Statistics, vol. 20, no. 89 (December, 1970).

60 Gore: "Sex, Martial Status and Suicide," 208.

61 Richard A. Kern, M.D.: "The Growing Problem of Suicide," *California Medicine,* vol. 79, no. 1 (July, 1953), 7.

62 *Lancet,* vol. 1 (May 24, 1952), 1059.

63 Leon Yochelson, M.D., ed.: *Symposium on Suicide* (Washington, D. C.: George Washington University Press, 1965), 18.

64 Jesus Rico-Velasco & Lizbeth Mynko: "Suicide and Marital Status: A Changing Relationship?," *Journal of Marriage and the Family* (May, 1973), 244.

65 Carlos Climent, Frank Ervin, Ann Rollins, Robert Plutchik, Catello Batinelli: "Epidemological Studies of Female Prisoners: IV. Homosexual Behavior," *Journal of Nervous and Mental Disease,* no. 164, (1977), 28.

66 Malvina Kremer and Alfred Rifkin: "The Early Development of Homosexuality: A Study of Adolescent Lesbians," *American Journal of Psychiatry,* vol. 126, no. 1 (July, 1969), 91–96.

Chapter 2
SCANDAL, BLACKMAIL & PUBLIC EXPOSURE, pages 25–34

1 Magnus Hirschfeld: *Die Homosexualität des Mannes und des Weibes* (Berlin:. Louis Marcus, 1914) as quoted in Jonathan Katz: *Gay American History,* 51.

2 The files of news clippings at the National Gay Archives, 1654 North Hudson Avenue, Hollywood, California, were the source of most of this documentation.

3 Other examples of similar suicides were found, including the suicide of Brandy Brent, the *Los Angeles Times* society columnist who killed himself following an arrest on morals charges (see the *Los Angeles Herald Express,* December 23, 1953); the suicide of a prominent pediatrician and Boy Scout leader arraigned on "six counts of child molestation" (see *Los Angeles Times,* December 20, 1949—"Dr. Burton, Accused Molester, Tries Suicide with Poison"); and the suicide of Jack McQuoid, who was arrested in Pasadena by a vice officer, and then blew his brains out (see *The Advocate,* April 7, 1968).

4 *Boston Herald American* (December 9, 1977), and Mitzel: *The Boston Sex Scandal* (Boston : Glad Day, 1980), 29.

5 *The Advocate* (November 8, 1972).

6 Larry Goldsmith: "Gay Man Commits Suicide After Arrest in Bar Raid," *Gay Community News,* vol. 9, no. 6 (August 22, 1981).

7 Lou Chibbaro, Jr.: "Suicide Results from Tyson's Corner Bust," *The Blade* (May 15, 1980); and Paul Wilcox: "Bigoted DC Courts Responsible for Gay Man's Suicide," *Workers' World* (May 23, 1980).

8 *The New York Times* (March 3, 1966).

9 Private correspondence with author (March 15, 1980).

10 Sasha Gregory Lewis: *Sunday's Women* (Boston: Beacon Press, 1978), 78.

11 Information on the suicides of Charles Montgomery and his lover was obtained through correspondence with Sarah Montgomery (May, 1980–December, 1981). For information regarding dual suicides see Marshall Schwartzburt, et al.: "Dual Suicide in Homosexuals," *Journal of Nervous and Mental Disease,* vol. 155, no. 2 (August, 1972), 125–130. For further information on Charles Montgomery and Sarah Montgomery, see *Gay Community News* (December 13, 1975).

12 For full documentation of the impressive work of this committee and the results of these efforts see Mitzel: *The Boston Sex Scandal* (Boston, Glad Day, 1980).

13 The press response to King's disclosure merits substantial documentation and analysis. It ranges from tabloid sensationalism ("Billie Jean: We Were Lovers," *New York Post* [May 2, 1981]; "Billie Jean: Had Lesbian Affair," *New York Daily News* [May 2, 1981]) to feature stories and analysis ("The Case of Billie Jean King" by Peter Axthelm in *Newsweek* [May 18, 1981]; "Why and When and Whether to Confess" by Lance Morrow, in *Time* [May 18, 1981]; *People* cover story [May 25, 1981]) to critical response from lesbians and feminists ("Match Point" by Katherine Triantafillou in *Gay Community News* [May 23, 1981], and "Court Gestures: Billie Jean Serves the Press a Coming-Out Story" by Anita Diamant in *Boston Phoenix* [May 26, 1981]).

Chapter 3
LESBIAN & GAY YOUTH AND SUICIDE, pages 35–48

1 The popular song recorded by Bobbie Gentry gave no indication why Billy Joe killed himself. When the song was developed into a movie, an incident involving a sexual experience with another man was included and used as Billy Joe's primary motivation for suicide. See Vito Russo: *The Celluloid Closet* (New York: Harper & Row, 1981), 142–143.

2 An interesting viewpoint on the subject is provided by David Rothenberg: "Teenage Suicides," *Gaysweek* (January 8, 1979), 18. See also James Knight: "Suicide Among Students" in H. L. P. Resnick, ed.: *Suicidal Behaviors* (Boston: Little, Brown, 1968), 230–231; and "Suicide and Homosexuality," *Playboy* (June, 1967), 174.

3 C. J. Frederick: "Trends in Mental Health: Self-destructive Behavior Among Younger Age Groups," *DHEW Publication No. (ADM), 76-365,* 1976.

4 See "Why a Surge of Suicide Among the Young," *U. S. News & World Report* (July 10, 1978): "Teenage Suicide: It Doesn't Have To Happen," *Co-ed* (January, 1980); "Why Some Children Elect To Die-and Do" by Lois Pinnick, *Boston Globe* (August 10, 1978); "Children Who Want To Die," *Time* (September 25, 1978); "Why Suicide?" by Michele Kamisher, *Boston Sunday Globe* (April 2, 1978); "Trouble in an Affluent Suburb," *Time* (December 1978).

   The recently published book, *The Urge to Die: Why Young People Commit Suicide,* by Peter Giovacchini, M.D. (New York: Macmillan, 1981), contains absolutely no references to youth suicides related to homosexuality. Francine Klagsbrun's *Too Young To Die* (Boston: Houghton Mifflin, 1976) includes a few references to homosexuality, yet fails to give adequate attention or analysis to the issue.

5 Private conversation (May 16, 1979).

6 Alan P. Bell and Martin S. Weinberg: *Homosexualities* (New York: Simon & Schuster, 1978), 454.

7 Marcel T. Saghir and Eli Robins: *Male and Female Homosexuality: A Comprehensive Investigation* (Baltimore: Williams & Wilkins, 1973), 276.

8 Dr. Klaus Thomas: "Suicide and Sexual Disturbances," *International Congress of Medical Sexology* (Paris, 1974), unpaged.

9 Robert S. Liebert: "The Gay Student Movement: A Psychopolitical View," *Change* (October, 1971). I thank Allen Young for bringing this article, as well as his own response which appeared in the Winter, 1971–72 issue, to my attention.

10 Ann Landers: *Ann Landers Talks to Teenagers About Sex* (Englewood Cliffs, N. J.: Prentice-Hall, 1968), 81.

11 A. Warren Stearns, M. D.: "Cases of Probable Suicide in Young Persons Without Obvious Motivation," *Journal of the Maine Medical Associa-*

tion, vol. 44, no. 1 (January, 1953), 16. Similar cases discovered through my research include the suicide of Albert Small, age 15, in Los Angeles, as reported in the *Los Angeles Mirror* (June 3, 1954); Ian Mervis, an Eagle Scout, 15 years old, who killed himself while "practicing knots," as reported in the *Los Angeles Mirror,* also on June 3, 1954; and the death of William M. Rohn who hung himself after dressing in a blond wig, black lace lingerie, a girdle and a taffeta dress, just two days after his wedding. Rohn left a note saying, "I finally have found the courage to end a horrible nightmare life," *Los Angeles Mirror* (May 5, 1954). These suicides reveal the need to investigate both transvestism and bondage as they relate to suicide. See R. E. Litman: "Psychological-psychiatric Aspects in Certifying Modes of Death," *Journal of Forensic Science, vol. 13, no. 46 (1968).*

12 William Robbins: "A Brilliant Student's Troubled Life and Early Death," *New York Times* (August 25, 1980).

13 Personal correspondence with Stuart Kellogg (December 6, 1981).

14 *NewsWest* (January 20-February 3, 1977), 5.

15 Personal correspondence (April 11, 1980).

Chapter 4
SUICIDE AND ACTIVISTS, pages 49–72

1 See Tim Cwiek: "Lesbian Activist Commits Suicide," *Philadelphia Gay News* (January 11–24, 1980), and *Sinister Wisdom,* no. 13 (Spring, 1980), on Claudia Scott. For coverage of Michael Silverstein's suicide, see Larry Tate: "Concerning the Death of Dr. Michael Silverstein, Gay Activist and Friend," and an additional article by Vince de Luca in *The Body Politic* (June, 1977), cover story, 10–11, as well as *The Crusader* (San Francisco, undated clipping [March, 1977?]).

2 Norman L. Farberow and Edwin F. Schneidman: "Statistical Comparison Between Attempted and Committed Suicides," *The Cry for Help* (New York: McGraw-Hill, 1965).

3 Phyllis Chesler: *Women & Madness* (New York: Avon, 1972), 45. See also Kathryn K. Johnson: "Durkheim Revisited: Why Do Women Kill Themselves?" in *Suicide and Life-threatening Behavior,* vol. 9, no. 3 (Fall, 1979), 145-153.

4 Chesler: *Women & Madness* 49.

5 Biographical information on Claudia Scott taken from a variety of sources: Frances Hanckel and Susan Windle, eds.: *Lesbian Writer: Collected Works of Claudia Scott* (Tallahassee, FL: Naiad Press, 1981), vii-ix, as well as the initial draft to the book's introduction; a memorial flyer which was produced and distributed by "The

Friends of Claudia Scott"; an interview with Frances Hanckel (New York City: December 22, 1980) and correspondence (October 28, 1980, December 27, 1980, January 30, 1981) and phone conversation (December 16, 1981). Also see Frances Hanckel and John Cunningham: *A Way of Love, A Way of Life* (New York: Lothrop, Lee and Shepard, 1979), 49-40, 53 (photo of Claudia on 51).

6 Quotations taken from the journals are dated whenever possible. The journals are in the possession of Susan Windle and I thank her for giving me access to them. Claudia left over a dozen volumes of journals in spiral notebooks that document her life from her teenage years to her death. The journals provide a remarkable record of one woman's development and the growth of a lesbian-feminist identity.

7 Claudia Scott: *Portrait* (Chicago: Lavender Press, 1974).

8 *Lesbian Tide* (October, 1974), cover and 23.

9 All quotations from Frances Hanckel are from the interview with her in New York City on December 22, 1980.

10 In *Sinister Wisdom,* no. 4 (Fall, 1977), Claudia wrote a letter entitled "'Confessional' Writing" (72-74) and stated: "I have no use for confessional writing. It bores me. There is a difference between life and literature, and I don't want to give up either, but I also don't want to confuse them." See her collection of poems from this period: Claudia Scott: *In This Morning* (Chicago: Tree Frog Press, 1979).

11 Interview with Laurie Barron, Marcy Muldawer, Susan Windle and Wendy Galson on February 21, 1981, in Philadelphia. All subsequent quotations from these women are also from this interview.

12 See *Sinister Wisdom,* no. 4 (Fall, 1977), 62, 103; *Sinister Wisdom,* no. 5 (Winter, 1978), 12–13, 103; *Sinister Wisdom,* no. 8 (Winter, 1979), 30, 72-74, 95; *Conditions,* no. 6 (Summer, 1980), 24-25, 241. Claudia's work appeared in other volumes of *Conditions,* but I was unable to locate these volumes.

13 Claudia Scott: "Rejection Slip Collage," in Frances Hanckel and Susan Windle, eds.: *Lesbian Writer,* 52-53. The artistic collage of rejection slips is in the possession of Susan Windle.

14 Hanckel and Windle, editors: *Lesbian Writer,* 98.

15 Information from Tim Cwiek: "Lesbian Activist Commits Suicide," *Philadelphia Gay News* (January 11–24, 1980), and interview with Frances Hanckel (New York City, December 22, 1980).

16 "Dr. Michael Silverstein Takes Own Life," *The Crusader* (San Francisco, undated clipping, [March, 1977?]).

17 Biographical information on Michael Silverstein is taken from a variety of sources: Larry Tate: "Concerning the Death of Dr. Michael Silverstein, Gay Activist and Friend," *The Body Politic* (June, 1977), 10–11, and the accompanying article by Vince de Luca; autobio-

graphical articles by Michael Silverstein, including "An Open Letter
to Tennessee Williams" and "The Politics of My Sex Life" from
Karla Jay & Allen Young, eds.: *Out of the Closets* (New York: Douglas,
1972); "The History of a Short, Unsuccessful Academic Career"
from Joseph H. Pleck and Jack Sawyer, eds.: *Men and Masculinity*
(Englewood Cliffs, NJ: Prentice-Hall, 1974). For a patronizing,
homophobic and poorly researched portrait of Silverstein (useful as
an example of the ways in which heterosexual men twist our lives
and our deaths for their warped purposes) see Leonard Kriegel: *On
Men and Manhood* (New York: Hawthorn Books, 1979), 163–166.

18 "The History of a Short, Unsuccessful Academic Career," in Karla Jay
and Allen Young, eds.: *Out of the Closets,* 108 (hereafter listed in
notes as "The History of a Short . . . Career" with page number). See
also Silverstein's "Power and Sex Roles in Academia," *Journal of
Applied Behavioral Science* (no. 8, 1972), 536-563.

19 "The History of a Short . . . Career," 109.

20 Larry Tate: "Concerning the Death of Dr. Michael Silverstein, Gay
Activist and Friend," *The Body Politic* (June, 1977), 10 (hereafter
listed in notes as "Concerning the Death" with page number).

21 "An Open Letter to Tennessee Williams," in Karla Jay and Allen Young,
eds.: *Out of the Closets,* 69 (hereafter listed in notes simply as "An
Open Letter" with page number).

22 "The History of a Short . . . Career," 111.

23 "The History of a Short . . . Career," 116.

24 "The History of a Short . . . Career," 117.

25 "The History of a Short . . . Career," 118.

26 Larry Tate: "Concerning the Death," 10.

27 "The History of a Short . . . Career," 118.

28 "The History of a Short . . . Career," 119.

29 "The Politics of My Sex Life," in Karla Jay and Allen Young, eds.: *Out of
the Closets,* 270 (hereafter listed in notes simply by title of article and
page number).

Silverstein was aware of the contradictions between his political
beliefs and his sexual attractions and discussed these contradictions
in this article. While stating, "Although I would never reduce anyone to a sex object, this fantasy attached itself mainly to young
pretty boys" (p. 270); he is also able to admit, "Even though I know
other gay men in the same situation, the same trap, even though we
know we need each other to make our lives worth living, we're still
too afraid of each other, afraid the other will take more than he'll
get. I am still afraid of my brother's needs. He is still afraid that I'll
despise him if I see how weak he feels. And it's still pretty boys that
give me an erection." (p. 274)

30 Interview with Allen Young in Boston.

31 "The Politics of My Sex Life," 271.

32 "The History of a Short . . . Career," 121.

33 "The Politics of My Sex Life," 272.

34 "An Open Letter," 70–72.

35 "The Politics of My Sex Life," 274–275.

36 Larry Tate: "Concerning the Death," 10.

37 Vince de Luca, untitled article in *The Body Politic* (June, 1977), 11.

38 Quoted by Larry Tate: "Concerning the Death," 11.

39 Quoted by Larry Tate: "Concerning the Death," 10.

40 I expand on this idea in a speech I presented at the memorial service for David Brill, a friend and cohort from the *Gay Community News*. The service took place while debate still raged concerning the controversial nature of Brill's death: "I find anger an appropriate response to a murder, but I am tempted to react to suicide with feelings of ,confusion and pity. I have to catch myself because I know the suicide of a gay person—any gay person—is ultimately no different than the murder of a gay person. A culture that hates us and conspires to eliminate us from society uses many tactics to accomplish its goal. It will first try to make us invisible, by withholding access to the media, by intimidating us with violence so we pass as straight on the streets, by denying we exist in every class, every racial group, every region of the country. When we fight our invisibility, they try another tactic—they say that we're sick, or sinful or outlaw. They make movies about us and show us as unhappy, wicked caricatures of human beings. Newspapers write about us as sexual perverts and society freaks and ignore us as a movement of loving people. When we continue to fight back and become a political movement to be reckoned with, this culture will use whatever force it can to rob us of our leaders, to intimidate us back into hiding. We are met with violence on many fronts—assassinations and murders of lesbians and gay men are only the most apparent example of this kind of violence. A society that forces a gay person into suicide by making life unbearable and ugly, by attempting to show to us that we are sick and evil and unworthy of life, and conspires to eliminate all of us from the world—by our own hands if necessary—is a society that engages in mass coercive murder. Suicide in the gay community is not a personal isolated action. It is the most pernicious strategy yet developed to achieve a genocidal end. It is an action spurred ahead by the realization that this culture has no place at all for lesbians and gay men . . ."

Similar thoughts concerning lesbian lawyer Margo Karle's death were written by Kevin Cathcart, see *Gay Community News*, vol. 9, no. 11 (October 3, 1981).

41 The tendency of friends and colleagues to blame themselves and their community for the suicide is a common, yet ultimately regrettable, response. Arleen Olshan, a friend of Claudia's, reportedly told *Philadelphia Gay News* that "It really bothers me that with all the support in the community something must still be lacking for this to happen. Somehow we're still not providing a space for people to talk about what's bothering them inside . . ." (January 11–24, 1980). At a memorial service for David Brill, Boston political activist Tom Reeves spoke of Brill's death as indicative of the local gay community's failure to support one another in the proper way. Reeves and Olshan verbalize the doubts and fears many of us are plagued with following a suicide.

42 For Don Miller see *The Advocate* (June 7, 1972). For Jan Sergienko see *Philadelphia Gay News* (December 1978), 14. For Terry Mangan see undated clipping from *The Advocate* in the vertical files at the National Gay Archives.

43 Sidney Abbot and Barbara Love: *Sappho Was a Right On Woman* (New York: Stein & Day, 1972), 44.

44 Jil Clark: "Margot Karle's Death: Questions Remain," *Gay Community News*, vol. 9, no. 11 (October 3, 1981), 3.

45 See Pat M. Kuras: "Political Analyst David Brill Dies," *Gay Community News*, vol. 7, no. 19 (December 1, 1979), 1, as well as "David Brill— In Memoriam," by Ellen B. Davis, Sheri Barden, Pat M. Kuras and Eric Rofes in the same issue, 5. Other information on Brill's death from *Boston Herald American* (November 17, 1979), *Boston Globe* (November 17, 1979), *Boston Phoenix* (November 27, 1979), *The Real Paper* (December 1, 1979). Notable subsequent coverage in the *Boston Globe* (November 27, 29, 1979), *Boston Herald American* (November 28, 29 and December 2, 15 & 31, 1979). For an article written by David Brill concerning suicide, see *Gay Community News* (February 14, 1976).

46 Phone conversation between author and unidentified Winthrop police officer, November 15, 1979 at 7:35 p.m.

47 Timothy Dwyer and Hank Klibanoff: "The Spiders and the Flies: Probing a Gay Murder," *Boston Globe Magazine* (April 13, 1980).

48 Interview with Sally Casper, February 16, 1979.

49 Interview, May, 1979.

50 Adrienne Rich: "Anne Sexton—1928–1974," in *On Lies, Secrets, and Silence* (New York: Norton, 1979), 122. The suicides of lesbians are not limited to Western culture. For an account of a dual suicide of two Indian women, see *Off Our Backs* (November, 1980).

51 Charley Shively: "Necrophilia As an Act of Revolution," *Fag Rag 29* (Boston, 1981), 7.

Chapter 5
SUBSTANCE ABUSE AND GAY SUICIDE, pages 73–88

1 Telephone interview, February 8, 1979.

2 Deborah L. Diamond and Sharon C. Wilsnack: "Alcohol Abuse Among Lesbians," *Journal of Homosexuality*, vol. 4, no. 2 (Winter, 1978), 123–142.

3 Leander Lohrenz, John Connelly, Lolafaye Coyne and Keith Spare: "Alcohol Problems in Several Midwestern Homosexual Communities," *Journal of Studies on Alcoholism*, vol. 39., no. 11 (November, 1978), 1959–63. See the following three notes also.

4 M. S. Weinberg and C. J. Williams: *Male Homosexuals: Their Problems and Adaptations* (New York: Oxford University Press, 1974).

5 R. F. Barr, H. P. Greenberg, M. S. Dalton: "Homosexuality and Psychological Adjustment," *Medical Journal of Austin*, vol. 1 (1974), 187–189.

6 Marcel T. Saghir and Eli Robins: *Male and Female Homosexuality* (Baltimore: Williams & Wilkins, 1973).

7 L. Fifield: "On My Way to Nowhere: Alienated, Isolated, Drunk: An analysis of gay alcohol abuse and an evaluation of alcoholism rehabilitation for the Los Angeles gay community" (Los Angeles: Gay Community Services Center, 1975).

8 Personal correspondence, January 19, 1980.

9 Information contained in this case study is taken from a series of interviews with the subject, 1980–1981.

10 Information on Allyn Amundson taken from articles in *Night Blooming: About Allyn Amundson,* Salvatore Farinella, ed. (Boston: Good Gay Poets, 1976).

11 Eugenia Parry Janis: "Remembrance," in *Night Blooming.*

12 Tom Farley: "Left Handed," in *Night Blooming.*

13 *Ibid.*

14 Salvatore Farinella: "Is There Life Before Death," in *Night Blooming.*

15 *Ibid.*

16 Dolores Klaich, talk delivered at University of Pennsylvania (Philadelphia) on February 25, 1975, reprinted in *Night Blooming.*

17 *San Francisco Chronicle* (August 28, 1980).

18 For information, contact The National Association of Gay Alcoholism Professionals, P. O. Box 376, Oakland, New Jersey, 07436. To obtain their Directory of Facilities & Services for Gay & Lesbian Alcoholics, send $2.50 to the above address. See also John Michael: *The Gay Drinking Problem. There Is a Solution* (Minneapolis: Comp-Care Publications, 1976); *The Way Back: The Stories of Gay and Lesbian Alcoholics* (Washington D.C.: Gay Council on Drinking Behavior, Whitman-Walker Clinic, Inc., 1981); Brenda Weathers: *Alcoholism*

and the Lesbian Community (Washington, D. C.: Gay Council on Drinking Behavior, 1976); Thomas O. Ziebold and John E. Mongeon: *Ways to Gay Sobriety* (Washington, D. C.: Gay Council on Drinking Behavior, 1980).

Chapter 6
AREAS FOR CONTINUED RESEARCH, pages 89–109

1 The only substantial information located by the author is on the suicide of Jack Lira, a Hispanic man and the lover of the late San Francisco Supervisor Harvey Milk. See "Supervisor Milk Finds Friend Dead," *San Francisco Examiner* (August 29, 1978); "In Memoriam: Jack Lira," by Don Amador, *Coast to Coast Times* (September 29, 1978); and Randy Shilts: *The Mayor of Castro Street, The Life and Times of Harvey Milk* (New York: St. Martin's Press, 1982).

   The Samaritans of Boston have produced a handbook focusing on the special needs of people of color in suicide prevention. See Elaine Gross: *Minority Outreach Project Handbook* (Boston: The Samaritans, 1982).

2 See Don Leviton: "The Significance of Sexuality as a Deterrent to Suicide Among the Aged," *Omega* vol. 4, no. 2 (Summer, 1973), 163–174, and W. A. O'Connor: "Some Notes on Suicide," *British Journal of Medical Psychology*, vol. 21, no. 3 (1948), 221–228.

3 Biographical information in this section from Allen Young: "Marshall Bloom—Gay Brother," *Fag Rag*, no. 5 (Summer, 1973); and Ray Mungo: *Famous Long Ago* (Boston: Beacon Press, 1970). Mungo's book "is dedicated to Marshall Irving Bloom (1944–1969), who was too good to be also wise. Some months after I completed this manuscript, Marshall went to the mountain-top and, saying, 'Now I will end the whole world,' left us confused and angry, lonely and possessed, inspired and moved but generally broken."

4 See Ray Mungo: *Famous Long Ago* (Boston: Beacon Press, 1970), and Steve Diamond: *What the Trees Said.*

5 Young: "Marshall Bloom—Gay Brother," 6.

6 Judith Coburn: Letter to the Editor, *The New York Times* (May 19, 1973).

7 Young: "Marshall Bloom—Gay Brother," 6.

8 *Ibid.*

9 David Eisenhower: "In Memory of Campus Activism," *The New York Times* (April 30, 1973).

10 Judith Coburn: Letter to the Editor, *The New York Times* (May 19, 1973).

11 Young: "Marshall Bloom—Gay Brother," 6.

12 Notes from a conference with Dr. Robert A. Litman, in the archives of the Institute for Sex Research, Bloomington, IN (July 23, 1969).

13 Calista V. Leonard: *Understanding & Preventing Suicide* (Springfield, IL: Charles C. Thomas, 1967), 304.

14 Barbara Smith and Beverly Smith: "Across the Kitchen Table A Sister-to-Sister Dialogue," in Cherríe Moraga and Gloria Anzaldúa, eds.: *This Bridge Called My Back—Writings by Radical Women of Color* (Watertown, MA: Persephone, 1981), 124–125.

15 Of note are: Robert Davis: "Black Suicide in the Seventies: Current Trends," *Suicide and Life Threatening Behavior*, vol. 9, no. 3 (Fall, 1979); C. Black: "Suicide Among Black Americans," in D. B. Anderson and L. J. MacClean, eds.: *Identifying Suicide Potential* (New York: Behavioral Publication, 1969), 25–28; R. H. Seiden: "A Study of the San Francisco Suicide Rate," *Bulletin of Suicidology*, vol. 1 (1967), 1–10; Herbert Hendin: "The Psychosocial Dimension," *Suicide and Life Threatening Behavior*, vol. 8, no. 2 (Summer, 1978); E. Reingold: "Black Suicide in San Francisco," in F. Wylie: *Suicide Among Black Females* (Washington, D. C.: Black Women's Community Development Foundation, 1974); Calvin Frederick: "Current Trends in Suicidal Behavior in the United States," *American Journal of Psychotherapy*, vol. 32, no. 2 (April, 1978), 172–200.

16 Robert Davis: "Black Suicide in the Seventies: Current Trends," *Suicide and Life Threatening Behavior*, vol. 9, no. 3 (Fall, 1979), 131.

17 Herbert Hendin: "Suicide: The Psychosocial Dimension," *Suicide and Life Threatening Behavior*, vol. 8, no. 2 (Summer, 1978), 105.

18 Robert Davis: "Black Suicide in the Seventies: Current Trends," 131.

19 *Ibid.*

20 Alan P. Bell and Martin S. Weinberg: *Homosexualities* (New York: Simon & Schuster, 1978), 450.

21 Vickie M. Mays: "I Hear Voices But See No Faces—Reflections on Racism and Women-Identified Relationships of Afro-American Women," *Heresies*, no. 12 (New York: Heresies Collective, 1981), 76.

22 Jesus Rico-Velasco and Lizbeth Mynko: "Suicide and Marital Status: A Changing Relationship?," *Journal of Marriage and the Family* (May, 1973), 241. They cite Jack P. Gibbs & Walter T. Martin: *Status Integration and Suicide* (Eugene: University of Oregon Books, 1964).

23 Herbert Hendin: "Black Suicide," *Archives of General Psychiatry*, vol. 2, no. 4 (1969), 28.

24 *Ibid.*

25 Herbert Hendin: "Black Suicide," 31.

26 Herbert Hendin: "Black Suicide," 33. Hendin's book on this subject, *Black Suicide* (New York: Basic Books, 1969), contains a chapter "Suicide and Male Homosexuality" which appears to be as uninformed as his article.

27 Chris Albertson: *Bessie* (New York: Stein & Day, 1972), 120–121.

28 Allen Young: "Out of the Closets, Into the Streets," in Karla Jay and Allen Young, eds.: *Out of the Closets* (New York: Douglas, 1972), 16.

29 Interview with Sally Casper (February 16, 1979).

30 Biographical information regarding Matthiessen and Cheney primarily from Louis Hyde, ed: *Rat & The Devil: Journal Letters of F. O. Matthiessen and Russell Cheney* (Hamden, CT: Archon Books, 1978). Other information from John Garraty and Edward James, eds.: *Dictionary of American Biography*, Supplement 4, (1946–1950) (New York: Scribners', 1974), 559–561; Giles B. Gunn: *F. O. Matthiessen: The Critical Achievement* (Seattle: University of Washington Press, 1975); *Harvard University Gazette* (November 18, 1950); George Abbott White: "Have I Any Right in a Community That Would So Utterly Disapprove of Me if It Knew the Facts," *Harvard Magazine* (September-October, 1978).

31 Quotations from the letters are from Hyde: *Rat & The Devil.*

32 Hyde: *Rat & The Devil,* 17–18.

33 Hyde: *Rat & The Devil,* 29.

34 Hyde: *Rat & The Devil,* 87.

35 Hyde: *Rat & The Devil,* 124.

36 *Dictionary of American Biography*, Supplement 4, (1946–1950), 560.

37 Hyde: *Rat & The Devil,* 241.

38 Hyde: *Rat & The Devil,* 246–247.

39 F. O. Matthiessen: *American Renaissance: Art & Expression in the Age of Emerson and Whitman* (London: Oxford University Press, 1941).

40 Hyde: *Rat & The Devil,* 355-356.

41 Kenneth S. Lynn: "F. O. Matthiessen," *The American Scholar,* vol. 46, no. 1 (Winter, 1976–1977), 91.

42 Hyde: *Rat & The Devil,* 365.

43 *Boston Herald* (April 6, 1950).

44 *Dictionary of American Biography,* Supplement 4 (1946-1950), 561

45 *National Cyclopaedia of American Biography,* Vol. 41, 1956 (James White & Co.), 396.

46 *Boston Sunday Globe* (April 2, 1950), 36.

47 *Boston Herald* (April 1, 1950).

48 Lynn: "F. O. Matthiessen," 92.

49 Brian MacMahon and Thomas Pugh: "Suicide in the Widowed" in *American Journal of Epidemiology,* vol. 81 (1965), 23-31. For a tragic example of suicide by a gay male "widow" see Lou Chibbaro, Jr.: "Double Tragedy," *The Washington Blade* (March 19, 1982).

50 Dan Leviton: "The Significance of Sexuality as a Deterrent to Suicide Among the Aged," *Omega,* vol. 4, no. 2 (Summer, 1973), 164. The death of Prescott Townsend, known in Boston as "The World's Oldest Practising Homoseuxal," provides an example, it appears, of an elderly person committing suicide. *Fag Rag* (Summer, 1973) reported that, "It appears to have been a case of his having chosen to die, since one source reports that P. T. [Prescott Townsend] had refused food and medication for his last few days."

Chapter 7
ENDING GAY SUICIDE, pages 110–124

1 See Appendix 4.

2 See Edwin S. Shneidman: "Suicide," Edwin S. Shneidman: *Death: Current Perspectives* (Palo Alto, CA: Mayfield, 2nd ed., 1980), 416–434 for more information.

3 See Brian MacMahon and Thomas Pugh: "Suicide in the Widowed," *American Journal of Epidemiology,* no. 81 (1965), 23–31.

4 Author observation at funeral.

5 Program from "David P. Brill Memorial Service," November 27, 1979, held at the Arlington Street Church in Boston.

6 Information from program "Memorial Service for Claudia Scott," April 20, 1980, and interview with Laurie Barron, Marcy Muldawer, Susan Windle and Wendy Galson on February 21, 1981.

7 Thomas S. Szasz, M.D.: *The Myth of Mental Illness* (New York: Harper & Row, 1974), 48–49.

8 William H. Grier, M.D. and Price M. Cobbs, M.D.: *Black Rage* (New York: Bantam, 1968), 150–151.

9 Viktor E. Frankl: *Man's Search for Meaning* (Boston: Beacon Press, 1962), 16.

10 Bruno Bettelheim: "The Holocaust—One Generation Later," Bruno Bettelheim: *Surviving and Other Essays* (New York: Knopf, 1979), 99–100.

11 See, in particular, Jonathan Katz: *Gay American History* (New York, Thomas Y. Crowell, 1976); Andrea Dworkin: *Woman Hating* (New York: Dutton, 1974); Mary Daly: *Gyn/Ecology* (Boston, Beacon Press, 1978); Heinz Heger: *The Men With the Pink Triangles* (Boston: Alyson, 1980); Lillian Faderman: *Surpassing the Love of Men* (New York: William Morrow, 1981); Vern L. Bullough: *Homosexuality: A History* (New York: New American Library, 1979).

12 Sidney Abbott and Barbara Love: *Sappho Was a Right-On Woman* (New York: Stein & Day, 1972), 14.

13 James L. Stoll, M. Div.: Testimony presented to the California Legislature, Senate Committee on Health and Welfare, Subcommittee on Medical Education and Health Needs. Hearing regarding Suicide, University of California, Los Angeles, April 6, 1974. Text located at the Institute for Sex Research, Bloomington, Indiana.

14 Jack Gibbs and Walter Martin: *Status Integration and Suicide: A Sociological Study* (Eugene, OR: University of Oregon Books, 1964), 55.

15 Frankl: *Man's Search for Meaning,* 78.

16 Rudy Kikel: "After Whitman and Auden: Gay Male Sensibility in Poetry Since 1945," *Gay Sunshine,* no. 44/45 (Tenth Anniversary Issue, 1980), 36. Kikel cites "doom" in the writings of Ginsberg, Rechy, Genet, O'Hara, Norse, Wieners, Williams and Burroughs.

17 John D'Emelio: "Dreams Deferred," *The Body Politic* (February, 1979), 26. D'Emelio's three-part essay on gay organizing before Stonewall provides an important account of the limited options available to gay men and lesbians in the 1950s and 1960s.

18 See Michelle Cliff: *Claiming an Identity They Taught Me To Despise* (Watertown, MA: Persephone Press, 1980) for an interesting and painful account of this experience from a lesbian of color.

19 Sally Casper interview (February 16, 1979).

APPENDIX 1, pages 127–129

1 David M. Robinson: *Sappho and Her Influence* (New York: F. A. Stokes, 1932), 29.

2 Biographical information from *The McGraw-Hill Encyclopedia of World Biography* IX (1973), 405; John Arthur Thomas Lloyd: *Sappho: Life and Work* (London: Arthur L. Humphreys, 1910); William Smith, revised by Charles Anthon: *A New Classical Dictionary* (New York: Harper & Bros. 1850).

3 Joseph Addison: *The Spectator,* 223 (November 15, 1711).

4 Arthur Weigall: *Sappho of Lesbos: Her Life and Times* (New York: F. A. Stokes, 1932), 26.

5 Weigall: *Sappho of Lesbos,* 26.

6 Denys Page: *Sappho & Alcaeus: An Introduction to the Study of Ancient Lesbian Poetry* (Oxford: Clarendon Press, 1955), 144.

7 Dolores Klaich: *Woman + Woman: Attitudes Toward Lesbianism* (New York: William Morrow, 1974), 133–148.

8 William Mure: *A Critical History of the Language and Literature of Ancient Greece* (London: Longman, Brown, Green & Longmans, 1854), 2nd ed., vol. III, 286–287.

⁹ Weigall: *Sappho of Lesbos*, 306–309. Weigall's description of Sappho's suicide is melodramatic to the point of high camp: "She was seized with panic. In a frenzy of terror and despair, she made the quick decision to kill herself, and, running like a mad thing across the grass, she flung herself from the cliff's dizzy edge, and fell to her death in the blue waters far below." (page 308)

¹⁰ William Smith, revised by Charles Anthon: *A New Classical Dictionary* (New York: Harper & Bros., 1850), 638, 773.

¹¹ John Arthur Thomas Lloyd: *Sappho: Life & Work*, 175–176.

¹² T. G. Johnson: *Sappho: The Lesbian—A Monograph* (London: Williams & Norgate, 1899), 51. For an important critical essay on Sappho by a woman, see Judith P. Hallett: "Sappho and her Social Context: Sense and Sensuality," *Signs: Journal of Women in Culture and Society*, vol. 4, no. 3 (1979), 447–464.

APPENDIX 2, pages 130–132

¹ Tim LaHaye: *The Unhappy Gays* (Wheaton, IL: Tyndale House, 1978), 40.

² Anita Bryant: *The Anita Bryant Story: The Survival of Our Nation's Families and the Threat of Militant Homosexuals* (Old Tappan, NJ: Revell, 1977), 96.

³ Paul Cameron: "A Case Against Homosexuality," *Human Life Review*, vol. 4 (Summer, 1978), 39–49.

⁴ Cameron: "A Case Against Homosexuality," 42.

⁵ LaHaye: *The Unhappy Gays*, 58. See also Murray Norris: "There's Nothing Gay About Homosexuality," *Christian Family Renewal Newsletter* (Clovis, CA); and William Rodgers: *The Gay Invasion: A Christian Look at the Spreading Homosexual Myth* (Denver: Accent Books, 1977).

⁶ Daniel Cappon: *Toward an Understanding of Homosexuality* (Englewood Cliffs, NJ: Prentice-Hall, 1965).

⁷ Letter to the editors, "Torture, Homosexuality and the Cry for Hope," *The Other Side*, 13 (April, 1977), 6. Cited in Letha Scanzoni and Virginia Ramey Mollenkott: *Is the Homosexual My Neighbor?* (San Francisco: Harper & Row, 1978).

APPENDIX 4, pages 135–136

¹ Sally Casper interview (February 16, 1979).

² Correspondence with Terry S. Gock, Clincial Coordinator, Suicide/Crisis Intervention Telephone Service Program of Life Crisis Services, Inc., St. Louis, Missouri (February 6, 1980).

3 Sally Casper interview (February 16, 1979).

4 Correspondence with James W. Toy, Coordinator and Trainer, Gay Hotline, University of Michigan (January 24, 1980).

5 Correspondence with L. Wiseblood, Coordinator, Lincoln (Nebraska) Gay Crisis & Referral Line (January 17, 1980).

6 Correspondence with James W. Toy, (January 24, 1980).

7 Correspondence with William Gronwald, Administrator, Gay Switchboard of New York (January 10, 1980).

8 A book that should become required reading for all hot-line counselors is A. Elfin Moses and Robert O. Hawkins, Jr.: *Counseling Lesbian Women and Gay Men* (St. Louis: C. V. Mosby Co., 1982).

INDEX

Eric E. Rofes was raised in Commack, NY, and graduated from
Harvard College. He works as a teacher and co-director of a private
school in Cambridge, MA. He writes, lectures and gives workshops on
a variety of youth issues including youth depression and suicide,
divorce and children, and teenage sexuality. Eric is the editor of *The
Kids' Book of Divorce,* a bestseller written by his students, which has
received international attention and acclaim.

In addition to his work with young people, Eric is a political activist who has worked on gay, feminist and other progressive issues. A
national organizer of the 1979 March on Washington for Lesbian and
Gay Rights, Eric has written for various gay and progressive papers,
including *Gay Community News, The Advocate,* and *The Guardian.*

Grey Fox Books

Daniel Curzon — *Human Warmth & Other Stories*

Guy Davenport — *Herakleitos and Diogenes*
The Mimes of Herondas

Edward Dorn — *Selected Poems*

Lawrence Ferlinghetti — *The Populist Manifesto*

Allen Ginsberg — *Composed on the Tongue*
The Gates of Wrath: Rhymed Poems
1948–1952
Gay Sunshine Interview
(with Allen Young)

Robert Glück — *Elements of a Coffee Service:*
A Book of Stories

Howard Griffin — *Conversations with Auden*

Richard Hall — *Couplings: A Book of Stories*
Three Plays for a Gay Theater

Jack Kerouac — *Heaven & Other Poems*

Stanley Lombardo — *Parmenides and Empedocles*

Michael McClure — *Hymns to St. Geryon & Dark Brown*

Frank O'Hara — *Early Writing*
Poems Retrieved
Standing Still and Walking
in New York

Charles Olson — *The Post Office*

Eric Rofes — *"I Thought People Like That*
Killed Themselves"—Lesbians,
Gay Men & Suicide

Michael Rumaker — *A Day and a Night at the Baths*
My First Satyrnalia

Gary Snyder — *He Who Hunted Birds in His Father's*
Village: Dimensions of a Haida Myth
Riprap & Cold Mountain Poems

Gary Snyder, — *On Bread & Poetry*
Lew Welch &
Philip Whalen